MESSAGE TO THE WARRIORS

ISBN: 978-0-9785531-8-0

Akoben House
P.O. Box 10786
Atlanta, Georgia 30310

www.AkobenHouse.com

Printed in the USA by
Morris Publishing
3212 East Highway 30
Kearney, NE 68847
800-650-7888

To

JALIYAH

Acknowledgements

I humbly say Meda ase pa to Odumankoma, the Abosom and the Nananom Nsamanfo who have nurtured my mind within a Warrior's spirit and given that spirit a victorious vision of Afrikan sovereignty. Every word herein is gratitude and prayer for this gift.

Meda ase pa to Yaa Mawusi, my complement and core. She has encouraged and supported every effort I have made to better arm our Warriors standing on the frontline. All of worth in these words I share with her. Medowo pa.

We offer a special Meda ase pa to our investors, Ayo Joyce Drayton, Pamela Kolade Wynn & Elijah Kambon Mann, Morro & Virgestine Sanyang, Erika Graham, Kibwe Biko, Jon Overstreet, Danny Akinbobola Donaldson, Demiko & Martina Aiken, Kwame & Akosua Radford, Nefertari Kimathi & Irritated Genie of Soufeese, Nyeasha Bethea, Adiama Yatunga, Natacha Rene, Kweli Mungu Mayasa (Bro. True) & Malkia Mayasa, Jomo Mutegi, Jasira Montsho, Bomani Mayasa, Omowale Mayasa and Sanyika & Makini Anwisye. The spirit of generosity they express toward the community is the way Afrikan people have always created reality. We have always selflessly supported those efforts which uncompromisingly speak to our ancestral memory, power and vision. And, because what this collective of individuals has done to ensure that this writing is published is explainable only through this spirit, it must be understood that what they have done lies beyond human appreciation.

I am indebted to the Irritated Genie for awakening

the idea of writing this book in me and for the support and resources offered to accomplish this task.

Kweli Mungu Mayasa (Bro. True) has been of enormous assistance in gathering and suggesting epigraphs for these chapters. Though the selection is mine (so he is not responsible for those which may seem inappropriate or inadequate), he was responsible for bringing many of them to my attention. The value of his working knowledge of our revolutionary spoken word to this project remains priceless.

The Zulus, Shaka, Aisha and Nic, have again and again and again sacrificed their time, energy and resources to help create a user friendly environment within which I could more easily do this work. Asafo Kweku Opare was instrumental in formatting both this book's text and cover for its printing. And Brother Nati of Afrikan World Books and Everyone's Place has gone to great lengths, lengths which speak to the exemplary quality of his character, in allowing me to not have to focus on other literary concerns while this book was being written. It is the heart of his spirit which motivates those who fall within his circle.

TABLE OF CONTENTS

Introduction

We fear for the thing we no see
We fear for the air around us
We fear to fight for freedom
We fear to fight for liberty
We fear to fight for justice
We fear to fight for happiness
We always get reason to fear

Fela Kuti

This book is about you, warrior. It's about the standard that has been set for you by our Ancestors. It's about the height that you must rise to in order to honor them, and gain and maintain the respect of your fellow warriors.

We are at war. And, because these hostilities will continue for some time to come, it's about the mentality and power you must have in order to be able to bring your children up in the warrior's way.

Understand that we are warriors, not soldiers. There are political, mental and spiritual differences between the two. Specifically, there is a clear difference in the depth at which the righteousness of the battle is internally understood by warrior and soldier.

On the one hand, warriors are at war for the liberation of their people because they have no choice, whether they want one or not. They are spiritually charged with liberating their people from the pain inflicted on them by oppressors. The role of the warrior is understood.

On the other hand, soldiers fight for the thrill of killing, or another's ambitions, or the need to survive financially. Generally, the soldier's cause is his employer's cause. The justness of the cause is irrelevant (whether or not soldiers have psyched themselves into believing their cause is just). Soldiers believe in their leaders in the same way that house negroes believe in their masters. They do not think for themselves as to cause and effect. Like slaves, they fear questions. And "too much fear creates slavery" (Swahili proverb). They are historically and ourstorically unaware. They do what they are told.

Mercenaries are a special variety of soldier. They are almost always fighting for someone else's cause and could care less about their target, even if it is one of their own. Some mercenaries can easily be defined as psychopathic in their thought and behavior. Killing is their first and greatest passion.

Given that combat is a natural part of the warrior's existence and that war is the root word of warrior for good reason, if we wanted to be simplistic, we could say that warriors, because they kill in battle, are soldiers. But it is not a given that a soldier is also a warrior. Warriors, in our tradition, also study who they are and what they must build when the fighting ends.

In terms of their outward behavior, warriors are fearless because there is no room for trepidation in a war to permanently arrest the assault against family/community/nation. They do not compromise. Warriors do not attack or exploit innocents. They are gentle with their own. Warriors respect the work of their Ancestors and Elders.

They are primarily defensive in their natural posture. Their primary function is to protect their people, excluding the treasonous. Their military functions only become offensive only when they must take the battle into the spaces of those who initiated the confrontation. Throughout his or her existence, the warrior is prepared for any exigency, military and otherwise.

Some might call this a nationalist's handbook, a warrior's workbook, a nationbuilder's manual on the basics of how to successfully confront this genocidal assault against our people. They are right. It is all of these. It is a tool to empower you on the frontline of battle.

We are in this conflict, but we are not responsible for it. We did not cause it. It was brought to us. This being the case, in order for us to be at peace with ourselves, it is an insult we must return with greater force than it was (and still is being) given. But, to do this, we have to know the nature of both the attack and the attacker.

Many pretend they know the way, but do not. Obviously, the majority of us are in serious need of guidance. If not, we would not still be having this discussion. Only a pacified fool would argue that we're not in deep, deep trouble. And, unless we've misread both our enemies and most of our people, there's no visible end of it in sight. No one who is conscious enough to be even vaguely aware of our situation as a battered, broken people should have a problem admitting just how bad our situation is.

An objective consideration of a problem's strength and magnitude opens the way to finding real, effective solutions to it. In other words, if you are able to recognize how difficult a problem is, then you will have a better understanding of how much energy you will have to dedicate to putting an end to it. And this is why we are here – to get a better idea of just how bad our situation is so that we will know how to permanently fix it.

With that said, we have been under continuous assault from a whole host of destroyers for over two thousand years. And, for all intents and purposes, this attempt to remove us from existence has been quite successful. Do not be fooled. Just because we physically operate in this reality does not mean we are here mentally.

Just look around. Most of us have degenerated into scattered, broken, fearful, selfish, disconnected, hunted, hounded, lost, visionless, invisible, self-hating super individualists who want love from anyone but those who look like us.

Even our idea of community has been distorted to fit the destruction coming from outside and festering within. Community, as a conscious, active, involved self/group-definition, has lost most of its everyday unifying force. In fact, when talking about us, most who use it still use the word community only to help others better control us.

We definitely do not act like a group of people who value each other. The health, lives and future of those we claim as part of our "village" have become less and less of a primary concern. We loudly shout to the world that we deserve the respect given men and women but fail miserably at providing for and protecting our most valuable resources -- our children.

4

If we are the warriors we believe we are, we have to stop here, at least for a minute, and honestly admit our faults. Otherwise, there is no need to continue this conversation.

We can also look around and see that many who loudly claim to be Afrikan nationalists are no different than those who talk community but claim that race is irrelevant. The deception is shameful. They have fooled themselves and each other long enough. Time is running out.

Those of us who know better have every reason to be alarmed. There is no law in the Universe which says that Afrikan people cannot be removed from existence or, worse, live the death of re-enslavement. And we say this while recognizing that most of us are still on the plantation. It is obvious that countless Afrikans have never stopped being mental, physical and spiritual slaves of a people who are no more than the living dead.

Nothing is an acceptable excuse for not stopping and reversing our steady movement toward even greater, more willful, self-hatred and destruction. Not even the ignorance and fear of punks will suffice. In that those who know but do not do are the most guilty, there are especially no excuses for those who claim consciousness.

However, that is not to imply that the bravest among us do not have serious challenges. So, before beginning, we have to give serious thought to how we can better turn ourselves into a battle-ready vanguard. Only a disciplined self-respect can give us the ability to march toward the frontline and successfully defeat our enemies. Only an uncompromising knowing and courage will enable us to build a powerful nation for our people out of the ashes of our destruction.

Before moving on to the heart of this matter, we need to make a quick note on terminology. Though Afrikan will be used most because it refers to both our appearance and original culture, it and Black will be used when referring to us. Both refer to the spirit and depth of our Ancestors.

Also, nationalist, nationbuilder and warrior will be used interchangeably when we are specifically talking to and about those who are consciously working to build us a sovereign Afrikan nation. And, of course, whether using Afrikan or Black, we are describing the type of nationalist we are working to become. Each indicates which people the nationalist belongs to and whom he or she has loyalty and accountability to before any other.

Therefore, unless otherwise indicated, as far as we are concerned, all five terms, Afrikan, Black, nationalist, nationbuilder and warrior, are describing the same person. By themselves and together they speak to the character of every individual who has seriously dedicated her or his life's energy to saving our people from any and all who would dare think to mistreat us.

european, white, yurugu, enemy and alien will all also serve the same purpose in identifying those who are not us. These names will be used to label those who have done all in their power to pacify and remove us from this planet.

asians and arabs are no different. History tells us they are as much enemies as Europeans. So far, though, they have just not been as successful in globally exploiting and oppressing Afrikan people as europeans. This is the only reason they are not our primary focus.

Hopefully, many will read this book. However, given what has already been said, only some will understand it for the revolutionary tool that it is. Even fewer will have the courage and will to act on what only conscious minds can be called on to do.

With that said, let's begin this discussion by defining just what is meant by nation, nationalism and nationalist.

Nation

Before defining what an Afrikan nationalist is, we need to know what we mean by a nation. It only makes sense that there can be no true nationalists without a nation. Well, at the least, they would have to have a good idea of what needs to be built and defended to create one. Without a working knowledge of what a nation is, anyone with the potential to be a nationalist would have no idea what they are driven to destroy or create.

Visions can only be crafted out of what we know and can imagine. What we think we want must be conceived before it can be achieved.

Of course, nationbuilding requires more than just some abstract, theoretical ideas. And this is true no matter how well they are able to describe in words what we believe we need. It demands individuals who have the courage to believe it is possible for us to build and defend a strong, respected nation. Such warriors must have the conviction to see our people as independent, powerful and sovereign.

Without question, vision and builder go hand in hand. Independence, power and sovereignty, *and* those willing to work to gain and keep them alive for their people, are basic to any definition of nation.

A nation is an identity. It is a people's way of telling themselves and others who they are. It is a progressive, evolving living tradition, a timeless story. It is a people's tried and tested way of life and the hope of extending that way into the future for as long as they exist. It is to our nation which we pledge unqualified allegiance.

Furthermore, a nation is a race of people who have created a culture in their own image. Races have different personalities and create different realities to serve their specific needs and imperatives. They hold different perspectives which they consciously use to build societies that reflect their different personalities. Racial differences are clear and meaningful. They go far beyond any simple "we're all human" argument.

It is only because of the european's criminal use of race to misdefine us as inferior and them as supreme that we do not want to think in racial terms. It is interesting, though, to now hear them loudly proclaiming that there is "only one race, the human race." But we know that this is only an effort to put awakening warriors back to sleep. Their wailing is no more than an effort to defend themselves from those of us who are no longer fooled by the lies denying or defending their psychopathic, racist thought and behavior as normal and human. Only now that we have exposed them for what they are do they want to hide their genocidal crimes behind our "humanity."

Races do exist. And there is absolutely nothing wrong with this. The biological, social, cultural and spiritual differences that divide us are to be treasured, not hidden or dismissed. Race and culture cannot be separated. Therefore, for Afrikan nationalists, to say race is to say nation.

In short, a nation is a people, a people who see themselves as one. Such a people have shared interests based on a common, core spirit, bloodline and experience in this world.

Though when we think of nationhood in this way we are speaking of millions of people, numbers are not critical to its definition. How many there are is not nearly as important as the depth of their spiritual, biological, cultural and social connectedness. Nations are one in countless ways.

So far we have been using "us," "we" and "our" when referring to nationalists and nation. For some, this may require clarification. It needs to be understood that Afrikan people are our only interest here. However, because we are only speaking to and about Black folk, there may be some confusion about exactly who we are referring to for those in the heat of battle who see little around them but self-loathing, mentacidal Afrikans, Afrikans whose minds have been turned against themselves and us, Afrikans who want nothing to do with "us."

Therefore, because we are speaking about us as *a people*, some potential nationalists may wonder about those who look like us but who do not consider themselves Afrikan and do not want to be connected to us in any meaningful, permanent way. It is a contradiction we find among our people throughout this society, as well as around the world, but among no other people.

There are many who look like us and have the same origin and ourstory but in no way see themselves as having any common interests with Afrikan people. They do not see us as one. Obviously, as a people, we remain unable to unite ourselves around a "Race First" philosophy like that taught by honorable Ancestor nationalists like Marcus Mosiah Garvey.

However, even though this glaring contradiction may seem to weaken our definition of nation, it is not a significant obstacle for nationalists. Our vision is far greater and higher than the confusion we see in the weakened minds around us.

9

Nationalists know the reason for this confusion. We are aware of *history* or "his-story" (the european's interpretation of past events) and *ourstory* or "our-story" (our understanding of the same dates, events and other social phenomena). We know what others have done to us as well as what we have allowed others to do to us in creating this confusion. We recognize the contribution of both them and us to the difficulty many of us have in recognizing and embracing our natural connection to every other member of the Black nation.

We also know that we have long been at war with those who would make us their eternal slaves. More importantly, though, we know that we have never stopped fighting against any and every alien invader who tries to destroy the minds, bodies and spirits of Afrikan people.

Still, we know that there are those who look like us but fight against us. And we are painfully aware that they are the majority of us at this point. Generally speaking, we recognize the presence of two basic types of Afrikans who have chosen not to work for our people (and to not work for us is to work against us).

One group is the lost souls. They are those whose ignorance of self and fear of others who they know kill without reason is far too deep for them to even think of doing anything about it. It would require an enormous amount of time and energy for them to accept their membership in the Black nation. It would take them even longer to act on this fact.

And, then, there are the negroes. These individuals are the ultimate, chronic self-haters. They can be described as the "truly vanquished" -- those who believe we did and should have lost the race war. They believe that our only salvation lies in becoming raceless, cultureless individuals absorbed to the point of invisibility by those they consider the victors. Often, these defeated, lost souls work harder to destroy us than even our enemies do. They will *never* work on behalf of our people.

Neither should trouble nationalists. We know that there are casualties in every war. This is unavoidable.

In this psychological war against a conscious Afrikan identity, we know that the memory loss and confusion over who we really are is the direct result of our enslavement, dehumanization and learned self-hatred. We know that this assault against our humanity has produced a number of us who will die denying their Afrikanity. So, we understand why these victims believe there never was and never can be such a thing as an Afrikan nation.

These casualties are mentacidal -- their minds have been turned against them and us. They are brain dead, out of their Afrikan mind zombies, determined to corrupt and/or destroy anyone who looks like them who is still sane. And, as such, they are willfully vanquished.

They have made a choice. They are firmly committed to treason against us and our Ancestors. And, because of this, they are lost to our war effort. They cannot help us and we have no time or need to worry about them, unless they indicate a desire to learn/change.

No matter who they are to us, we cannot allow them to distract us from the work we must do as Black nationalists. We are the vanguard. We cannot afford to be contaminated from within.

Is this a racist agenda? Some potential warriors have been confused by the propaganda saying that Black nationalists are racist. They wonder if we should not just release our righteous rage and embrace an easier life of some "new world," "post-racial" (interracial) after party.

11

Those who have not fallen too far into this self-defeating trap should know that it is not possible for an Afrikan nationalist to be a racist. Racism is a group action, not an individual one. The acts of individuals of one group against the individuals of another are only successful if they are supported by the power, approval and support of the group to which they belong. And this power, approval and support must come from an aggressively dominant group. As such, any accusations of racism must be assessed at the national, not individual, level.

Afrikans, as a group, do not have the kind of power required to act against europeans. We cannot even act against ourselves without their approval. But, of course, that approval was readily given long ago. Viewed in this context, we are not and cannot be racists.

Certainly, you will hear many different arguments attempting to make Afrikans into racists. However, these are only the acts of mentacidal individuals in service to another people's power. They are not acting of their own accord. The mentacidal never do. They are unaware of their own accord. They can only operate on behalf of those who own and control their minds.

Like zombies on murderous missions for their masters, such individuals are acting out of the power of the white mind over them. To think otherwise would be to accept that what a slave thinks is a product of his or her own mind. But we know better than this because our Ghanaian Ancestors taught us, "The slave's wisdom is in the master's head." And, from this insight, we can logically conclude that so are his or her words and actions.

Without white power controlling their thought and action, they would never think or behave in these ways. Without ignorance of self and fear of what would happen to

12

them if they did not act against us in service to the white nation, no Afrikan would act against another Afrikan solely because they are of the same race.

These are not racists. These are powerless, needy, vanquished, fearful individuals operating in the shadow and under the protection and guidance of the white nation. Their consciousness and will are ruled by a nation of insecure beings which single-mindedly pursues its interests. They operate within the psychology of a warped, psychopathic, racist mind whose survival interests require the suppression, destruction and genocidal elimination of Black people.

Racism *must* be fully reconceptualized as a strategy of white-on-Black war. It is a war that is no different than any other Europeans have waged against others. In all of these wars against people of color, they have never been able to succeed without the assistance of traitors. Our traitors, whether consciously or not, see Europeans as all powerful and are more than willing (in the weakness of their self-hatred) to allow that malicious power to be channeled through themselves against their own.

Collectively or otherwise, neither negroes nor lost souls have any power of their own. It is definitely not collective, a condition which is fundamental to any scientific definition of power. They are too afraid of yurugu's wrath to want to know each other as political allies. So, they have no power.

These puppets are not racists. They are merely agents, lower level managers, proxies of someone else's. They are merely the instruments of racists.

Neither are nationalists prejudiced against europeans, or anyone else we have defined, through historical contact and study, as enemy for that matter. In

13

order for us to be prejudiced we would have to know nothing about them because prejudice means to judge without knowledge. But we do know them. We have more than ample proof of who they are and what they have done. There is a major difference between a blind hatred and a righteously enraged awareness. Afrikan nationalists are only acting on what we already know to protect ourselves from further harm.

Those unable or unwilling to judge europeans (and others) beforehand, based on the historical record, will continue to be "surprised" and caught off guard because of their conditioned belief in the humanity of those who are destroying them. Their inability to use a people's historical record to judge them individually and together will leave them, time and time again, slaughtered on the killing fields of the race war.

Nationalism

Nationalism is having a great love and sense of loyalty and patriotism for one's nation, for one's people. It is an ultimate love of self because you are your people. The more deeply you love them, the more deeply you can appreciate yourself. More than anything else, nationalism is an expression of the heart.

As social creatures we should know that love for self should never override the love one has for one's nation/people. It is only through our people that we truly exist. As our Ancestors said, "I am because we are, and since we are therefore I am."

No man wins or loses alone, except those who live outside a human reality. Any win or loss affects and is affected by others.   Everything is defined within a context. And, for people, that context is each other.

Nationalism is a way of life.   It is the politics of any self-loving people.   It is the creed of nationalists.   It is the most fundamental political reason for our existence.   We live for our nation.   And, as Afrikans, our potential for that is what makes others fear us so much.

Nationalism puts race first.   Because, as we have already said, to say nation is to say race.   Black nationalists do not distinguish Afrikan people from the Afrikan nation. We do not see ourselves as separate or separable any more than we see europeans as identifiable apart from the white nation.

That "individual first" propaganda of europeans is promoted so that we will wrongly believe that in society the individual is considered more important than nationhood. This not now, and has never been, true.   And believing this lie keeps us blind to the fact that our loyalty is really to europeans as a nation.   Many of us have even taken it so far as to believe that this is "our" nation and not theirs alone.

There is no "we" in white nationalism.   There is nothing Afrikan about it.   It is only they.

Whoever is making the final decisions tells us who is running a society.   And we're not talking about their mouthpieces like their president or some other actor. We're talking about those who own and control this reality. And that includes all of them, from the point when they came into power until today.   We are not limiting our sight to this present time.

Understood in this real way, it is the european who has the power, the final decision-making power in all areas of people activity.   This is a european dominated country, not "ours."   And warriors need to stop fooling around with

15

this truth, trying to find a safe place to play hide any awareness of our self-imposed powerlessness from ourselves and seek a hollow glory in this insanity.

As a people, we need nationalism. It is our most formidable psychological weapon against our enemies. It serves as a kind of social glue to unite us as a force our enemies cannot defeat as long as we know who we are. Nationalism is a tool of empowerment which provides a direct path to sovereignty for those who know how to handle it well. In fact, nationalism is one of the most powerful weapons any people can have.

However, as with race, we have learned to view being nationalist negatively because we love other nations/peoples so much more than our own. We see nationalism as a "perspective" (a choice) which wrongly separates us from whites and others, when our greatest desire is to finally, lovingly be embraced by them.

Because of how europeans, arabs and asians have used nationalism against us, we see it as something bad and undesirable. And it is because their form of nationalism is racist and hateful that we have come to believe that there is no other kind.

In the same way, we cannot recognize that this nationalism against others is at the very heart and soul of white people. Blinded by their lies and our ignorance of self, we have passively come to see their nationalist racism and hatred as only short-lived episodes. We have even fooled ourselves into believing that their public expressions of racism are only the acts of a few misguided individuals. We want to blame an economic order, conveniently forgetting that it is a system created by them in their own sterile, gluttonous image, and say the "misguided ones" are only innocent individuals emotionally caught up in

16

desperate, corrupting capitalist circumstances.

Still, the greatest evidence of our weakness and submission to their claims of national superiority is seen in us accepting, without question, their teaching that nationalism is not a good thing for us.

But we, as Afrikan nationalists, must know better than to believe the truth of liars. Their historical record tells us all we need to see or consider. What they have done and continue to do against us should leave warriors with only one conclusion when thinking about members of the european, arab and asian nations: they are forever our "Bitter Enemy."

The successful outcome of any nationalist movement is sovereignty for the people. Being sovereign means having absolute control over the life of the nation. Right now, as always, for Afrikan people, sovereignty is measured by how intelligently, independently and powerfully we control our resources, story, culture, time, space and destiny. It is to have the power within the nation to control our lives and to control them in our best interests, regardless of opposition from outside.

Accordingly, being sovereignty has to mean that there is no one beyond us who makes any decisions about how we rule ourselves, how we live, what we believe, how we deal with enemies (whether aliens or traitors) and how we visualize our future and communicate and express that vision. It means that we are completely and consciously self-defining, self-determining and self-empowered. And, since no nation has ever risen to power and stayed there without holding their own traditions sacred, sovereignty necessarily means that we know, respect, protect and extend in time through every coming generation who we are as a direct reflection of our Ancestors.

17

Sovereignty is our ultimate goal. Needless to say, for us to be the kind of Afrikan nationalist warriors our people need, we must want sovereignty for Afrikan people more than we want to live.

So, when we talk about sovereignty, we are not speaking of the popular "sovereignty movement." That fad is about individualism, about feeling free while still under enemy occupation. We are about nationalism, actually being free as a people which would automatically make us into free individuals. We can quickly summarize this point by contrasting the Occupy and Sovereign Citizens Movements with Afrikan Sovereignty.

The Occupy Movement is the scheme of disgruntled europeans who are angry with their parents for creating economic problems that are making their lives difficult. This is no different from their parents' anger over the Vietnam War and sexual restrictions on open white sex in the 60s and 70s. These spoiled brats have no desire to get rid of the system. They simply want the freedom to live as they choose under the protection of this system. In other words, they want a larger share of the pie. They have no problem having us believe that this is "our" cause because our numbers strengthen their movement's success. But the Occupy Movement has absolutely nothing to do with us.

The Sovereign Citizens Movement among whites is designed to force their government to give them more individual and/or group sovereignty. They simply want to legally do whatever they please. For this reason alone, they argue that this government is illegal. And many of them are quite willing to be violent if threatened by its agents. But, in truth, the goal is not to dismantle the capitalist system or make it more equitable, if that were possible and they remain what they are. They only want to change places with the other whites who profit more from it.

The Sovereign Citizens Movement among Afrikans is about these individuals learning about the collection of illegal acts of yurugu's government. It, also, is not an effort to change the european's laws. They only want to use their contradictions against them (e.g., to get rid of debt, be exempt from taxation, claim abandoned/unoccupied property, etc.). These "sovereign citizens" want to become immune from legal prosecution.

Of course, in itself, the term sovereign citizen is self-contradictory. You cannot be your own government under someone else's rule. No society has ever allowed that without falling.

In our community, this movement is often spread through tricksters who con weak-minded and/or desperate individuals who are willing to pay ridiculous fees for classes. They believe these lessons will teach them how to declare themselves sovereign. It is a form of reactive, "safe sovereignty."

These escapists want to pretend that the openly disrespectful behavior Europeans have historically displayed toward others with impunity somehow does not apply to them. They want to believe that somehow, unlike through *all* of their existence, europeans will suddenly change their character and respect anyone's claims to sovereignty within european occupied and influenced space.

Whites have never respected the laws and treaties/agreements they have made with others unless those others had the military power to devastatingly retaliate. They have not even done this among their own. So, why would any Afrikan who is aware that europeans see them as their greatest threat, be foolish enough to believe that they would be respected without a means of enforcing their will?

The Afrikan nationalist warrior's goal of sovereignty is very different in its politics and vision. It is purely nationalist. Afrikans having this insight want to build a nation totally independent of all foreigners and their cultural influences. We want to operate strictly from an Afrikan center.

This is a movement to benefit a nation of people, not an individual here and there. Afrikans who cherish a vision of sovereignty want a completely separate space from whites. We want to establish and empower all of the institutions a nation needs, especially a military, for ourselves. And we want to only answer to ourselves (which would include not having to answer to the western controlled United Nations).

We are not about reforming babylon. We are about the business of revolution, a complete and total change, absolutely in our favor.

We do not react to our oppression, seeking to find some way of becoming a successful appendage to this pale insanity. We have no desire to celebrate some fake, dependent "sovereignty." We are acting to build an independent nation of our own.

Afrikan nationalists are not interested in doing anything which does not present the opportunity for them to further test and prove their accountability to Afrikan people. Conveniently misdefined, highly individualized "lifestyles" which claim a revolutionary consciousness do nothing but weaken the interpersonal obligations which strengthen our national bond. The various safe ways of survival through self-serving spiritualism, wholistic healthism, sovereigntism, etc., do little more than make us even more like the fragments our enemies need us to be to further shatter and scatter us so that we can be even more easily exploited and destroyed. These pretenses of identity allow Afrikans who naturally have a communal spirit to feign progress in an anti-Afrikan society through the arrogant worship of self.

Alien-oriented identities are without substance and inner strength. They do not require us to confront this vampire people and their decadent way of death which is progressively assaulting us from the outside and eating away at us from the inside. They allow invisibility and offer truly vanquished individuals a chance at the only peace and love they can imagine -- death.

In fact, playing around with these extremes reveals a personal weakness guided by a belief that we do not have the ability to create our own for ourselves. And this naturally leads us to conclude that the european way is the best of all possible ones. Consequently, our ultimate goal becomes to be even better at this individualistic game than them.

Through the eyes of Afrikan nationalists, sovereignty describes the *whole* social order of a nation. The production of great minds, safe, loving families, accountable government and the goods and services needed to keep each functioning properly is sovereignty's domain. For us, sovereignty must be understood in terms of complete control over a society's input (what raw materials come in), throughput (how it is processed) and output (what finished products come out).

The following chart can serve as an example of how sovereignty applies in those institutions essential to any people's survival.

Institution	Input	Throughout	Output
Education	students, educators & institutions	disciplining nationbuilding education	visionary knowledgeable thinkers
Family	complements, family & community	problem solving training	integrated frontline families
Spirituality	warriors & righteous spiritualists	traditional spiritual indoctrination	spiritually conscious "priests"
Politics	ideology, workers & masses	nationalist political instruction	involved grassroots organizers
Economics	resources, businesses & work ethic	communal business experience	motivated accountable entrepreneurs
Military	weaponry & military experts	martial skills training	prepared , dedicated warrior class

Now to further analyze the components of these sovereign processes:

Education

Input: Afrikan centered students, educators, curricula, libraries, books, videos and adequate funding to support enough independent institutions (operating with little to no overhead) to house and educate all Afrikans who want to build a new reality.

Throughput: actually educating children and adults in fully independent communal schools and colleges/universities in everything we need to survive and advance our people; practical application of skills in real life community settings and projects; rites programs for all ages providing knowledgeable instruction about each individual's coming roles and responsibilities, the creation and growth of an inter-communal comprehensive educational system that educates us from before birth to transition.

Output: disciplined minds, conscious warriors, accountable nationbuilders and committed Afrikan nationalists; graduates able and determined to contribute their time, energy and resources to build schools even better than those they attended; centered warriors and teachers of ourstory and definers of our future; individuals qualified in community and nation governance.

Family

Input: potential complements; children, Elders and respectful extended family members and neighbors; stable communities.

Throughput: purposeful, visionary marriage; responsible procreation; wise Elders consistently and intimately involved in the lives of their children and grandchildren; training and support for all age groups and in every area of family development.

Output: frontline complementary married warrior couples;

23

children reared to build nationbuilding families; worthy models of Afrikan familyhood; countless generations of Afrikan nationalist families.

Spirituality

Input: people with a desire to be spiritually connected to the Creator, their ancestors and themselves; warriors who want to better use their spirit as a weapon in this war.

Throughput: thorough, voluntary, non-proselytizing, full indoctrination into traditional Afrikan spiritual systems by priests (masters in our traditions) who know that we are at war.

Output: nation-serving spiritual warriors; righteously enraged warriors who are spiritually connected; warriors who know the god within as Boukman, Nat Turner, Denmark Vesey and Malcolm X did.

Politics

Input: communally grounded individuals and organizations motivated to work with and organize our people; warriors not distracted by electoral politics; an Afrikan nationalist ideology (set of guiding principles about how we need to do what we need to do now and our vision of the future based on a conscious warrior's understanding of history and ourstory).

Throughput: political education about the politics, ideologies and rhetoric of Afrikan nationalism.

Output: highly political, local grassroots organizations

uncompromisingly centered in our Ancestral truth and way; united individuals fully involved in producing positive, empowering, productive change in our communities around the world.

Economics

Input: massive quantities of resources; men and women with a mind for business and who have a serious work ethic.

Throughput: extensive training in pooling resources; progressive communal nepotism (training and hiring only our own); expansive bartering experiences; internalization of ethical, nationalistic good business practices.

Output: a cadre of networking individuals, strongly tied to each other in an effort to build an economic empire second to none; warriors who hustle for, not against, us – who do not see their own as prey.

Military

Input: able bodied potential warriors; adults and Elders with good mechanical and gunsmithing skills; instructors skilled in self-defense and military operations; educators with a vast working historical knowledge of the tactics and strategies of militaries worldwide.

Throughput: martial arts; weapons training; survival training; classes and videos on self and community defense; instruction in military science, especially guerrilla warfare.

Output: an army of individually capable warriors (each an

army in and of him or herself); fully defended Afrikan communities and mobile spaces; ample weaponry for every trained, able body in the community; fully functional battle plans at every level of society; Afrikans seen and feared as a credible threat by any intelligent individual/people who would consider attacking any one or all of us; a warrior class who defines itself as Afrikan, understand the concept of enemy and are able and willing to identify and confront others who deserve this label.

Bobby E. Wright taught us that the only way for mentacide to become rooted and eventually defended and championed by the mentacidal themselves is for it to become institutionalized. That is, in order for self-hatred and other-love to take on a life of its own among the target group members, they must be taught this in every institution that governs their lives. This is the case for Afrikan people.

Therefore, if we want to be free of this dependence-breeding slave mentality, we have to have complete control over those social institutions which generate and regulate our mental, physical and spiritual definitions of what is real and what is not. In any given institution, be it education, family, economics, religion, politics or military, every philosophy, practice, and vision must be under our *complete* control and guidance if we are to be free.

Nationalists

Nationalists or, rather, true Afrikan nationalists have devoted their lives to the unconditional liberation, empowerment and sovereignty of Afrikan people. True nationalists know their enemies, all of them. And while we know that the most immediate threat is from whites, we know that they are not even slightly our only ones.

Still, the presence of others does not lessen the fact that europeans are our primary foe. We know this because we know history. And history tells us that, compared to others, what they have done to remove us from the face of this planet and human memory has no rival.

The magnitude of what they have done should never be lessened. Their crime is against the Creator, not just humanity. This is an aggression which has imbalanced the Universe, not just us. In and of itself, this makes their offense far beyond human forgiveness and forgetfulness. It is immeasurable and incomparable in its viciousness, depravity, aggressiveness, deceitfulness, inhumanity, consistency and conscious intent. No other enemy comes close.

Given that we are nationbuilders with enemies, there can be no such thing as an Afrikan nationalist without a mission, goals and vision of sovereignty. All of these should be plainly spelled out in a mission statement.

As a very, very serious declaration of intent, this statement needs to be well thought out, well written and prominently displayed. It should be posted where it can be seen so that it will regularly remind us of who we are and the duties and responsibilities we have promised to ourselves, our nation and Creator.

The following is an example of a general Afrikan nationalist's mission statement:

As an Afrikan nationalist fighting to maintain my and my people's lives and sanity in this anti-Afrikan reality, I affirm the following:

1. *I will not be contradictory. What I think will be exactly what I say and what I say will be exactly what I do. I will uncompromisingly be who I think and say I am.*
2. *I will love and build with Afrikan persons of good will and character.*
3. *I will distinguish my wants from my needs and never emphasize the material above the mental and spiritual.*
4. *I will learn and teach our children ourstory. I will help them see and understand their power and their personal responsibility to use it in the best interests of Afrikan people. I will rear them to be Afrikan nationalists.*
5. *I will strive to be independent in every possible way and help my fellow warriors to be likewise.*
6. *I will respect my body and treat it like the temple it is. I will endeavor to elevate my martial skills to their highest potential and always be on guard for myself, my family, community and nation.*
7. *I will honor our warrior Ancestors only, using them at their finest as a model of the perfection to which I aspire.*
8. *I will never use derogatory, demeaning language against my Brothers and Sisters. I will always show them the utmost respect. I will speak to them in the race-nation spirit of family, knowing that we are one and that to curse them is to curse myself.*
9. *I will never confuse friend with enemy and will, without qualification, treat each accordingly.*
10. *I will live to remove enemies from my people's minds and spaces. I will work to secure all that is ours.*
11. *I will always remember to never forgive or forget what has been done to Afrikan people and do all I know and am able to do to stop this mentacidal, genocidal process now and never let it happen again.*

12. I will do all in my power to liberate, empower and make Afrikan people sovereign.

Every Afrikan nationalist's mission statement should resemble this. These declarations are serious personal plans of action. They should come from the depths of our heart and soul. They are not being written just to impress us with our ability to make warriorhood sound adventurous or decorate an otherwise blank wall. They are a warrior's promise, a blood oath to her- or himself, our living people, those of us yet to arrive, the Ancestors and the Creator.

In clear, concise terms this vision should be stated in the Afrikan nationalist's mission statement. In clear, precise ways this should be evident in the Afrikan nationalist's life.

Again, however, these are individual mission statements (even though there is every reason for Afrikan nationalist organizations to also have such statements). And, because we are individuals, each person's collection of affirmations should be custom composed to fit where they are in their development as a warrior. Accordingly, they should affirm what, in practical terms, they see as their current and immediate future work. It should go without saying that as the Afrikan nationalist's consciousness matures his or her mission statement should evolve accordingly

There is nothing out of the ordinary in setting such high standards as minimal requirements for Afrikan nationalists. Or, at least, they should not be seen as extraordinary. They should be looked at as what, at the very least, should be considered normal for those of us who realize what time it is and what we must do to liberate, empower and make our people sovereign.

In establishing this model for ourselves, there are many Afrikan nationalists whose lives are worth studying as examples of how normal Afrikan nationalists should think, speak, behave and build. When we speak of our most impressive Afrikan nationalists we are talking about uncompromising warrior Ancestors like:

- *Queen Nzingha* who refused to allow her people to be enslaved by turning her territory into a safe, protected space for them and any other Afrikans who were able to escape there;

- *Jean Jacques Dessalines* who led the Haitian Revolution, the first successful war of enslaved Afrikans in the western hemisphere. Like Nat Turner, who saw him as a model of what he needed to do, he was clear that every white on the Island must either leave or die;

- *Marcus Mosiah Garvey* who created the largest, most effective organization of Afrikan people on this planet ever, a movement solely directed toward the global unification of Afrikan people into a sovereign nation whose destiny was completely under our control;

- *Nana Akua Afriye (Mama Gerri)*, a premier Afrikan nationalist who educated herself in what was needed to open warriors' minds to their power and obligation to Afrikan people and started schools to train them. On the street and in closed meetings, she was equally determined to organize our people in a revolutionary way;

- *Queen Mother Moore* who was always armed. This outspoken woman was one of the strongest voices leading the movement for Afrikan nationalism, separatism and reparations;

30

- *John Henrik Clarke* who was the most profound ourstorian we've had. He helped millions of struggling warriors to understand in Afrikan centered terms the complexities and simplicity of a host of eurocentrically misdefined concepts including accountability, sovereignty, motherland, revolution, marxism, "discovery," leadership and obligation;
- *Khallid Abdul Muhammad* who set the standard of warriorhood for so many of our youth. A phenomenal orator, strategist and organizer, he stood as a brilliant Afrikan example of what being a man was all about in a world militarily determined to destroy our people;
- *Hannibal Afrik* who started a school, summer camps and youth and Elder rites programs all geared toward the production of fearless, knowledgeable, determined, focused warriors. His model of what a nationbuilder is, of what an Elder is, of what one who fights to free his people from this insanity every minute of every hour of every day for as long as he lives, is second to none in our revolutionary struggle.

Every Afrikan nationalist should be familiar with these giants and their work.

Even so, we must not limit our view of the models we choose to guide and elevate our minds to those whose names some of us already know. Many, many more whose names we have never heard have also worked above and beyond the call of duty in our communities around the world. Countless numbers still do.

So, while we remember and appreciate the genius, wisdom and power of these phenomenal men and women, we must never forget that they are merely the ones who were given the talent and mission of being foremost in our public eye. They are only the ones who were the most visible.   They are but the tip of a massive nationalist iceberg that goes back to the first invasion of the Continent.

The Warrior's Enemies

White nationalism is what put you in bondage
Pirate and vampires like Columbus, Morgan, and Darwin
Drank the blood of the sheep, trampled all over them with
Steel, tricks and deceit.
Nothing has changed take a look in our streets

Autum Ashante

In order to solve a problem you have to know its source. To state the obvious, our problem lies in how we see ourselves. We see ourselves as a powerless, inept, unoriginal people, whether it is in fact true or not, and it is not. And we act accordingly.

This neither negates nor denies the root cause -- european aggression, systematic exploitation and planned genocidal destruction. We would not be in this situation if it were not for them. This cannot be questioned.

Knowing the horror of our condition may make some of us uncomfortable, which may cause them to reject the truth of this statement. However, truth is truth, although the fear of acting drives many to love lies. Anyone who cannot see this or is in absolute denial of this fact has been wearing some seriously dense historical blinders.

As such, if we are again to become the powerful, ingenious, sovereign people we once were, we have to remove whatever shackles there are which restrain our minds, bodies and spirits. But, to permanently correct this, we have to know that these chains are not naturally there. We have to know that they were placed there on purpose so that we would remain oppressed, divided and more easily exploited.

In making this choice to be free, we have to identify who is doing this to us. We have to stop living in fear and put some serious thought into correctly defining enemy. For, if that enemy remains in power after the shackles are broken, there is a good probability that they will succeed in re-attaching them, this time more firmly. We are not dealing with idiots or beings who do not know exactly what they are doing. If we were, we would not be having this discussion.

Strictly speaking, an Afrikan nationalist's enemies are any person, living, dead or yet to be born, who in any way did, is or will work to prevent Afrikan people from being liberated, empowered and sovereign. It's not complicated. Anyone who thinks, says or does anything against our people or who is the friend of our enemies is our enemy.

Some would try to convince us otherwise. Some would say the enemy of my enemy is my friend. This ignores the fact that one can have multiple enemies and that these enemies can also war against each other while collectively warring against us.

Some even see befriending enemies as the solution to our problems with them. But doing this keeps them in power over us. If we truly understand the concept of enemy, why would any serious Afrikan nationalist possibly want to expend energy in a wasted attempt to turn an enemy into a "friend," except possibly to turn him or her into an agent against his or her own for us?

It makes no difference how young or old, what sex they are or how innocent they appear. Enemy is enemy. We are at war. War is needed to bring about revolution. Of this, our enemies are clear. Study revolutions throughout world history where people kill and risk their lives for the freedom to live as they desire. More importantly, read about the Haitian Revolution in Jedi Shemsu Jehewty's (aka Jacob H. Carruthers) *The Irritated Genie* and learn about Afrikan people's courage in fighting their enemies. Study the examples of Nat Turner, Queen Nzingha and Yaa Asantewa. Read and/or listen to Malcolm X, Khallid Muhammad and Kamau Kambon to learn their wisdom about dealing with enemies. Enemy is enemy.

Be a warrior scholar and do not believe the hype. There are no civilians in war. All are involved, whether they want to be or not. To do "nothing" is to work against us. There is no nonparticipatory option.

We must be clear on this, especially in our war. In this war there is only us and those who would kill us or assist in killing us. There is only us and those we must stop "by any means necessary" before they kill us. Being an innocent bystander is not an option. Silence speaks volumes against us. And inaction opens the back doors to our spaces for enemies.

Another point which must be made abundantly clear is that we are not fighting against enemies who can be contained or isolated from those of us who want to live in peace. We cannot forcefully banish them to europe or some heavily guarded island.

We are not dealing with enemies who are capable of understanding what love or humanity means. We are dealing with people who cannot be themselves without oppressing and taking from others. We are dealing with minds that cannot survive unless they can turn everyone else into carbon copies of their all-consuming, evil selves. And, for those caught up in the dream of humanizing evil, be not deluded. They have no choice other than to be themselves.

These albino creatures feel compelled, even divinely appointed, to invade every space they have not already violated. They have an uncontrollable appetite for corrupting anything that is innocent, to tarnish or stain anything that is new or they have not spawned, to taint anything that is clean, to blemish anything that is pristine, to pervert anything that is normal/natural, to disrupt or create chaos within anything at peace, to violate and fragment anything that is whole and has integrity and to kill anything it cannot change or control.

Afrikan nationalists do not operate on the assumption that our enemies have a conscience. As Bobby E. Wright clarified for us, europeans know the difference between right and wrong. They simply choose to ignore the difference.

Even if we wanted to, we cannot save europeans from themselves. The west is not salvageable. It is determined to create its pleasure out of others' misery. They have no choice and, for this reason, neither do we if we want to survive as a people. There is no reforming them.

Only revolution is reasonable. And by revolution we mean destroying what exists and building from the foundation up again. It is either them or us. There are no other choices.

Black nationalists understand this. Nevertheless, there are far too many Afrikans who have the potential to become members of the warrior class but who do not. We look around and see countless shells of Afrikans who are so confused over the enemy's identity that they are killing each other. It is an inbred ignorance of these truths which keeps so many of our would-be Afrikan nationalists treating each other as if we are our own worst enemy.

So, the problem is not that warriors do not know how to properly identify an enemy or to fight for whatever it is that they may want. The problems are with us correctly identifying who our true enemies are, determining what to fight for and knowing exactly why we want to fight for it.

Still, warriors can never forget that the enemy is not only outside of us. Enemies are both internal and external. The battle is against both the anti-Afrikan, self-hating insanity that is so comfortably nestled in our subconscious *and* the visible enemy of a nation of supremacist-aspiring individuals who created, populate and run this white reality. The battlefield is both in our minds and in this social environment.

However, because of the european's success at turning us against ourselves, the battle for self-love and Afrikan sanity is being waged more and more inside than outside our own minds. We can most easily see this fall from Afrikan grace in the elevation of the lower mind over the higher one in so many of us. The easy habits and weaknesses which turn us against ourselves have become firmly entrenched. We have even stooped to the point of convincing ourselves that this inferior mindset is the way we are naturally.

Therefore, we need to spend the bulk of this

discussion addressing the enemy within ourselves. However, to be fair, among Afrikans the enemy within is not only within Afrikan nationalists. There are also enemies roaming our community who look just like us. And because it is often necessary for us to operate hand-in-hand with those we serve, we must be aware of their issues also. They cannot be overlooked as we move toward a sovereign solution.

Because liberation is our mission and time is of the essence, Afrikan nationalists do not waste time arguing with other Afrikans who truly believe in their mentacide. Though it is a serious obligation for us to warn others through informing them of the way of this world, when we realize that they are not listening except to argue an enemy's side, we must stop wasting our time and energy on them.

Our Ancestors warned us that "association breeds assimilation." Accordingly, arguing with a fool will eventually turn you into one. As a rule of thumb in these instances, we should remember that small minds only deserve, and are usually only capable of comprehending, the simplest of responses. Give them no more than they are capable of understanding and, then, move on.

They also told us to, "give the warning; some will survive." This is what we do for those who do not know or want to know that they are the object of another's destruction. It is up to them whether or not they want to survive. Those who do not want to listen are not our problem. For the time being, those who are lost are lost.

Neither do we waste time in discussion with so-called conscious Afrikans who want nothing more than to argue, debate and disparage others for the attention and counterrevolutionary benefit they derive from that.

These debates and reactions do nothing more than direct our attention farther and farther away from concrete nationbuilding action. They involve arguments and issues that we do not have time to worry about. Our focus must remain on forging ourselves into disciplined, formidable centers within the conscious community.

There is no reasonable argument denying what has brought us warriors into existence. Therefore, there is no viable argument against our thinking, active presence in this time and place.

Furthermore, those claiming consciousness who are making these endless, distractive arguments have nothing concrete to offer in terms of nationbuilding. Their dreams hinge on rising up by hanging onto the coattails of those who have done years of serious thinking and work. They start "fights" so that they can finally be seen, not because those they attack have not provided quality leadership for us. If they had not been worthy models of Afrikan warriorhood, they would not have become targets. Some people are *only* able to get attention by attacking people who are known and honored.

We have to be smart enough to see through the loud, offensive voices and recognize the small minds behind them. You can see the limitations of their vision and natural talent in the activities they engage in and issues they support, such as white sex, bootlegging conscious Afrikan products and making alliances with enemies. No matter how they want to rationalize them, all of these practices morally and materially hurt our movement toward Afrikan sovereignty.

Insecure, weak individuals such as these are not trying to build a nation. They're doing nothing more than trying to find a stage where, finally, they can be seen.

Along with our responsibility to issue a warning, we

have to stand as viable options for those we have spoken to who are willing to listen and think. Afrikan nationalists must have the sense to see that talking without doing is a proven internal enemy. What difference does it make if you know everything about what is destroying you if you do nothing to stop it? Whether you want to call this place amerikkka, afairyka, babylon, hell or all of the above, it makes little difference if you are doing nothing more than critiquing it.

Truth, without the force of power, is meaningless. Afrikan nationalists must set the example by articulating the assault, stopping it and building what we need. All the while, we must remember to consistently remind ourselves that what has been done to us, and continues to be done to us, is much, much more than a crime against humanity. It is a crime against the Most High.

We must always remember this and know that there are no "bad apples" among europeans who unfairly give the rest of them an undeserved bad name. There is no single group of individuals within the white race who can be blamed for what they have collectively done. There is no omnipotent elite who can be separated from the masses and singled out for responsibility for their barbaric inhumanity.

These are a nation's crimes. And the white nation includes every single solitary european. All europeans are racists.

Recently, a "conscious" writer attempted to divide europeans into groups ranging from those who were openly racist to those who were not racist at all. She argued that those who did not actively work to hurt Afrikan people and/or who did not see us as inferior should not be defined as racist.

We beg to differ because all europeans, from the

materially wealthiest to the poorest, from the newest to the latest arrivals to these shores, reap the benefits of stolen property. The very spaces they occupy and claim as their countries, the places which feed and house them and which they so patriotically protect, were stolen from others.

The condition they live in on this stolen property is irrelevant. And, unlike what the media would lead us to believe, the majority do not live in deprived situations, especially in comparison to us or the other people their ancestors murdered in order to steal it. Even their hungry and abused benefit from having pale skin, if not materially then psychologically.

Those who receive stolen property, *according to their very own laws,* are as guilty as those who stole it. There has been an incredible transference of property through their generations. And the value of what was originally stolen has grown beyond calculation.

We must also remember that the genocidal method by which it was stolen is also inherited by those who continue to benefit from this murderous theft. The sins of the fathers and mothers are passed down to the sons and daughters. This is universal law.

Lineage, the bloodline, is the most important factor tying benefit and blame to the whites we see today. If we understand how lineage works, we know that *they are their ancestors,* just as we are ours.

Another point which speaks to the myth of the nonracist european is the mind of those Afrikans who have a burning desire to be close to them. Through a warrior's eyes, it is obvious that those whites claiming Afrikan "friends" only have these associations because of the severely mentacidal state of these so-called "friends." It is a mentacide physically and psychologically beaten into the

Afrikan mind over many generations of institutionalized racism and interpersonal racist terror. If it were not for their self-hating desire to be loved and validated by europeans (or anyone other than Afrikans for that matter), these individuals would in no way want to have european friends. They would understand the contradiction and treason inherent in such "friendships."

Of course, now that whites and their colored advocates have declared this to be a post-racial society, our yearning to be their friend works to their advantage. Today, having a "Black friend" is the best defense a racist can have against being labeled a racist. It makes the question, "How can a white with a Black friend be racist?" seem like a real one.

But no matter how we look at it, it is the Afrikan's mentacide, not the european's "humanity" or apology for his/her ancestors' wrongdoing, that causes them to seek out and accept the "friendship" of europeans. For, if they were not blindly running down amnesia inducing mentacidal paths, they would never have worked so hard to forget the unforgettable or forgive the unforgivable.

Knowing this, the only europeans who could possibly be nonracist would be those who are actively, genocidally working against their own. This would not be the only criteria however. He, she or it would also have to be making a conscious effort not to be "friendly" with any of us.

A final warning: Afrikan nationalists should be wary of Black (and white) marxists, whether they call themselves communists, socialists, scientific socialists or internationalists. They are all caught up in the belief that whatever class in the capitalist system we are a member of is much, much more important than our race. They see this battle for survival as one between those who own and control virtually every material thing of worth and those who work/slave for them. In other words, in their minds, the only important conflict exists between the haves against the have-nots, the upper crust and all beneath them and, globally speaking the so-called "Third World" against the "First."

Specifically, those who call themselves Black marxists, socialists, communists, etc., would have us believe that all Black people must work together with the white working class in this revolution against "our" exploitation by the elite. In their distorted, but highly politicized minds, elite is not synonymous with european. In order to win this revolution, they tell us that we must become one mass with yurugu's working class through accepting each other's differences.

Regardless of what these differences are, regardless of the fact that they are purely products of the white mind and are anti-Afrikan, we are told that we must defend and promote them for the sake of having greater numbers. Consequently, we are led to conclude that things which directly work against Afrikan interests, things like feminism, individualism and homosexuality, must be embraced in order to bring about this "revolutionary oneness."

By definition, marxists and those like them are violently anti-separatist (from yurugu) and aggressively hateful of nationalism, well, any form of nationalism except white nationalism. Historically, they are as racist as their capitalist brothers and want no more than to remove them from power so that they can replace them as the exploiting elite.

Afrikan nationalists believe in the power of numbers on the frontline, too. We also recognize the need for unification, but not with whites.

Still, we are clear on the impracticality of a majority of Afrikans operating as one at this time. The manufactured differences between us insures that any unification which includes the mentacidal could only be temporary. Blacks who love whites but hate themselves prevent the possibility of an Afrikan centered future.

Therefore, the Afrikan nationalist works to first strip Afrikan people of the vestiges and mutations of eurocentric thought and practice. Then, and only then, will unification naturally unfold.

We look to unite earnest, Afrikan centered warriors in our movement. We recognize that sovereignty is forged through clear, grounded minds who see Afrikan people in exclusive, unique, nationalist terms. We understand that you cannot build a nation with those who love themselves fighting alongside those who hate themselves and love our enemy (including those who fight the enemy only because they will not love us now).

On the battlefield this obviously poses a problem. But in a sovereign nation formed after victory, the long-term effects of this combination of Afrikan nationalists and those in love with our enemies would be catastrophic.

The Warrior's Behavior

The warrior's behavior toward other like-minded warriors ought to be looked upon as the light shining upon the hill for all to see...Those Brothas and Sisters who have yet or will not come into any realm of consciousness ought to at least see and admire our collective discipline

Brothas Keepa

We know ourselves best by what we think, say and do. In the same way, we know ourselves equally well by what we do not think, say and do. How we publicly (and privately) present ourselves is a major statement about what we think about ourselves and the vision we claim to pursue. We cannot separate ourselves from our mind, words, appearance or actions without being a serious contradiction within ourselves and in the eyes of those who look up to us.

To assist us in more effectively working to attain a noncontradictory order within ourselves and how we are seen within the community, the following chart is offered. It provides brief descriptions of the attitudes, beliefs and actions which should generally characterize the Afrikan nationalist. To further emphasize the importance of these qualities, they are contrasted with those self-hating

Afrikans display. A more detailed discussion of each category follows the chart.

	Afrikan nationalist	raceless zombie
STUDY	student for life; has a worthy library; knowledgeable of his- and ourstory; incessant, powerful thinker	reads little; studies nothing of worth; focuses on trivia; historically and ourstorically illiterate
WORK ETHIC	entrepreneur; hard worker; internally motivated to produce what our nation needs	lazy; externally/money motivated; job hunter/works for others
ORGANIZATION	centralized on the frontline; organizes life around nationbuilding mission/vision; oriented toward sovereignty of future generations	disarrayed (all over the place); without focus or direction; planless; no vision outside immediate image and survival
FAMILY	family/child-centered; married or committed; bears and rears own children; assists peers and those who are younger; stabilizes and improves marital relationships; extends self into the lives of all Afrikan	makes, but aborts, neglects, abuses and/or abandons offspring; lives to be single (serial monogamist – has multiple relationships one right after the other never seeking to learn what love is really about); irresponsible socially, economically, educationally to offspring;

	children	contributes little of worth to nuclear/extended family
LAND	land conscious; understands land-food connection; communal; knows that control and protection determine ownership	landless; no land aspiration; genuinely believes european/arab/asian space is theirs also
DISCIPLINE	internal; constantly self-aware of thoughts, words and deeds; ever working to hone/improve self; noncontradictory	external; oblivious to need for and benefits of self-restraint; without reasonable boundaries; dependent on instant gratification
HONESTY/ DEPENDABILITY	trustworthy; always there when needed; independently sees what needs to be done and acts accordingly	untrustworthy; chronic liar; appears when there is something to be gotten; pretends concern only to exploit
SPENDING/ CONSUMPTION	frugal; does not waste resources; does not waste money on fads; distinguishes wants from needs; avoids credit unless absolutely necessary; does not support alien/enemy businesses/economies; buys Afrikan; barters extensively	extremely wasteful; the ultimate super conspicuous consumer (buying to be seen); mindless materialism; works to spend; owns nothing of worth (renter, leaser); credit-dependent; fully supports alien/enemy businesses/economies

INDIVIDUALISM	individualism developed to serve greater good; power over self	individualism to benefit self; power over others
MORALITY/ ETHICS	based on universal order; highest possible rules; standard setting; modeling the best of righteous behavior; accountable to the Creator	based on selfish individualism; wrong only if caught; models worst of all possible behaviors; gets over on others by any means necessary mentality; operates without a working conscience
SPORTS/ ENTERTAINMENT	participation for fitness sake; focus on martial arts; laughter for relaxation; imagery for education and motivation ("edutainment")	obsessive distraction from work and responsibilities; childish escapism (distraction from reality); laughter to keep from crying
MUSIC	Afrikan Insurrection Music (AIM); warrior's classics; music with a conscious, revolutionary purpose	whatever is popular; the more vulgar, self-debasing, sexually and violently explicit and exploitative, the better
ATTIRE	moderate to conservative; functional; always wears something to reflect our ancestral connection	whatever is the latest, most revealing, most expensive styles; self-esteem wrapped up in popularity of clothes worn
ELDER REVERENCE	absolute respect; wisdom seeking; attentive to Elders'	none; Elders seen as useless burdens, as prey; preference for disloyal old

	needs; works to become an honored Elder	folk ("olders") when required
ANCESTORS	own; ancestorship awarded only through a life's record of service to family, community and nation; unworthy dead dismissed; offers libations daily	any dead but own (except those approved by others); veneration given based on record of willful compromise; libations seen as pagan
SPIRITUALITY	deeply connected; emphasis on higher mind/self; nonreligious; obeys higher mind; controls appetites; knows that the Creator is the only omniscient, omnipotent, omnipresent existence; knows the Creator is within	no true spiritual belief (spiritually disconnected); religious; emphasis on lack of self-control/lower mind (physical and material appetites); nothing is sacred
LEADERSHIP	leads by individual and family example; sets the standard; has a righteous vision grounded in our Ancestors	follower (even when appearing to lead); misleader pretending oppressor's ideals/goals are his/her own; unoriginal; visionless; profit/prestige driven
COMMITMENT	wholly dedicated; incorruptible; uncompromised; relentless; knowledgeably	fluctuates/unstable; follows whoever is in power

	dedicated to family, community and nation	
DRUGS & ALCOHOL	does not use, sell, transport or advocate using (to include any tobacco product) any chemical, natural or otherwise, that impairs/distorts normal human functioning	addicted; advocates addictions; lives for the high/stupor
GOSSIP	nonparticipant; always checks origin/source of hurtful/troubling statements	active participant; initiator and spreader of unverified statements; cares less about source or whom it harms
SEXUAL ORIENTATION & ATTITUDE	strictly heterosexual; sex primarily for procreation; sees sexual intercourse as sacred; sees womb and seed as divine	whatever is in vogue; whatever facilitates "success"; sex as a game of conquest (an accumulation/body count); sex-focused
LEVEL OF SERIOUSNESS & SOCIABILITY	battle ready; disciplined, mature adult; builds relationships; dedicates time to others	play oriented; an eternal, immature child; builds dependencies; seeks to use others
RACE CONSCIOUSNESS	believes in "Race First"; race is primary self-definition; sees race and culture as inseparable	seeks self-definition as anything but Afrikan; unable to comprehend race culturally, socially, politically or genetically

	culturally, socially, politically and genetically	
POLITICS	nationbuilder; works with like-minded builders; defines politics as the organization of people in the community around their interests and of holding community selected leaders accountable to them; nationalist-separatist; sovereignty-seeker	voter; solely focuses on electoral politics; unconcerned with accountability; believes the government operates with good will and is self-correcting; integrationist-assimilationist (focus on "breaking racial barriers")

Now, let's take a moment or two to further clarify the above descriptions of the inner thinking of Afrikan nationalists.

(STUDY) – Afrikan nationalists reserve a part of their day for reading, watching and listening to serious, revolutionary nationbuilding focused materials. Depending on the warrior's personality, this time should be equally divided between the study of political theory (how to organize people and to what ends) and the actual planning and practice of concrete action.

At minimum, warriors should allocate at least an hour of their best time to this. This "best" time is when the mind is operating at its optimal efficiency which, for many, is usually early in the morning, when it is most quiet and before the digestion of food begins to drain our energy, or before sleep, which allows the mind to mull over the material as one's body rests. An equal, if not greater, amount of our personal time should be spent quietly thinking about what we have studied.

The person who says, "I have read enough," but is not doing anything constructive in the community, obviously he or she has been reading the wrong material, has not read enough or has not given enough serious consideration to what has been read.

(WORK ETHIC) – Afrikan nationalists work. There is no other way to build a nation. Thought must be applied in the physical reality.

Of course, the most relevant question here is of what type of work we do. Other questions would be about who we do this work for and how much effort should we put into it.

On the question of what type of work, the answer is both simple and complicated. Simply speaking, as Afrikan nationalists, we do the work that we can do best. We do the work we were sent here to do. We do the work we were given the talent to do.

However, on the more complicated side of this question, no matter what talents we come with, if we are truly Afrikan nationalists, the nation determines how and where we use them. Whatever vocation we choose to pursue, it must be completely geared toward strengthening the national agenda and vision. There is no talent for which this cannot be applied.

In terms of who we do the work for, the ultimate goal is to work for self and people. This requires work that is not in service to nonAfrikans or that is dependent on the wages others control and dole out.

Of course, the last question, which asks about how

intensely Afrikan nationalists should apply themselves to the work they have been called on to do for our nation, should not have to be answered. Nothing less than our best effort will do. We are building under the watchful eyes of the Creator and in the tireless tradition of our Ancestors.

(ORGANIZATION) – An Afrikan nationalist's space, activities and relationships are all well organized. And it is an organization which reflects a future orientation, designed to be the most efficient possible and studied for error and weakness in order to be constantly improved. This type of organization is a process, a conscious effort on the part of warriors to better refine and focus their time, energy and thoughts as nationbuilders.

It is said that a disordered life reflects an unbalanced, jumbled mind. Therefore, there is little room in an Afrikan nationalist's life for the distractions confusion brings. There is too much work to do and too little time to do it in to waste time searching for thoughts and things which should readily be at one's fingertips.

This personal order also manifests itself in the nationbuilder's physical, mental and financial contributions to nationalist organizations. And it is an order that demands the creation of such organizations if they do not yet exist because the nationbuilder understands that power lies in ordered numbers.

(FAMILY) – Afrikan nationalists follow the tradition of their people. We look to our Ancestors for guidance as to what should be our foremost priorities recognizing that those who came before us are the wisest of us all. When we make the time to seriously do this, we see that one of the most important of our traditions is that of being family and child centered.

It is because we are who we are that we search for worthy complements to marry and, with those complements, work to establish safe, loving homes in which to rear the children we create. It is because we follow in the tradition of our Ancestors that we do all in our power to mold our children into strong, knowledgeable, committed, resilient Afrikan nationalists who understand their most important life's work as being and doing the same.

As we said, Afrikan nationalists are builders. And, in nation construction, building starts with the family. As we move forward, we must always remember that Afrikan nationalism is an intergenerational aspiration. It is not the achievement of any single generation. It is something we must work at for as long as we exist as a people. It is never finished. Therefore, it must be approached accordingly. It must firmly rest on a foundation of family first.

(LAND) – There is no nation without land. Unknown to some operating in the fantasy of another's matrix, cyberspace is not land. You cannot grow food or build or defend a physical house, community or state in cyberspace. Land is physical, tangible, usable for the actual mining of our resources and production of our needs.

After themselves, land is a people's first anchor in nationhood. Without it, there is no self-determination because you remain dependent on others for the resources for survival that only land can give.

Without land you are not connected to your ancestors because their remains and memory are increasingly distant. Your physical story is also out of sight and mind because you cannot see yourself in an alien environment. Only at home can the ground you stand on be completely familiar.

And, last but not least, protected, occupied land means sovereignty. Every true Afrikan nationalist's vision for his or her people is impossible without it because sovereignty means controlling one's space. If there is no sovereignty a people cannot exercise absolute control over their time, energy, beliefs, practices and material resources.

(DISCIPLINE) – Without discipline nothing of lasting value can be accomplished. Admittedly, we have chosen the most difficult work in any social reality. We have volunteered our services to rebuild a nation, virtually from scratch. We have to be more focused and self-controlled than others, especially those who see their mission as preventing an Afrikan nation from ever rising again. And greater strength requires greater discipline.

At the same time, a disciplined life does not come from the approval of others. It comes from approval of self. It is internally, not externally, formed and enforced. So, if we want true, lasting discipline we must discipline ourselves. We must continue to do what we are tired of doing, accept what others see as the impossible as a welcome, obligatory challenge and work at removing our weaknesses (the bad) until they are gone and increasing our strengths (the good) until they are second nature.

(HONESTY/DEPENDABILITY) – We must believe we can trust those on whose shoulders we stand and those with whom we stand shoulder to shoulder. Equally true, they must be able to naturally depend on us. This must be a demonstrated trust, a trust developed through the experience of mutually depending on each other, a record showing consistently positive, expected outcomes. It must have evolved through the practice of reciprocity, of mutual give and take.

(SPENDING/CONSUMPTION) – Thousands of years ago, Ptahhotep warned us that "He who is ruled by his appetite belongs to the enemy." europeans, arabs and asians can have nothing that we need. This does not mean that their resources cannot be exploited to our ends. In fact, that is within the nature of guerrilla warfare.

Also, we must not limit our imaginations by exclusively focusing our attention on the ego-salving, physically violent, combative fighting imagery that completely dominates the idea of warriorhood in the western media. Serious warriors know that in enemy territory guerrilla warfare is not waged only on the streets with artillery and in hand-to-hand combat. It is also incorporated into our day-to-day interactions with enemies and how we generally think, speak and act.

Regardless of situation and tactic, one of the primary advantages of guerrilla warfare lies in the taking and use of enemies' implements, weapons and other technologies against them. Still, we are only out to exploit others' technology and material advantages as they fit the designs of our initiatives. We do not want those who created or stole this technology in the first place. We do not want their culture, logic/reason or insanities along with what we take and use of theirs to advance our interests. We absolutely do not want to bring them along with their useable goods.

Generally, our goal is to control our "spending/consumption" because our national economy is based on us making what we need for each other and buying those goods and services exclusively from each other. If we must buy from non-Afrikans, we buy and spend the least amount possible. Race first must be our economic philosophy.

Furthermore, whether spending on each other or others, we consciously distinguish between wants and needs with needs taking the greater priority. We do not buy things so that we can be on finer display. We are not addicted to the latest style or gadgets. We understand the difference between them and those things which are functional and necessary for our nationbuilding work.

(INDIVIDUALISM) – While individual excellence should be applauded, individualism, "me"-ism, "I"-ism, that selfish, arrogant, self-centered way of putting oneself before all others is unacceptable among Afrikan nationbuilders. It is not characteristic of secure Afrikan people ourstorically. We are a communal people.

We work best as a collective because we love each other and know the power of the group. Certainly, we compete with each other. But it is not an envious, hateful, damaging competition. It is cooperative competition. Competing amongst ourselves is designed to sharpen our personal, Creator-given skills so that we can individually be the best in fulfilling our role within the warrior class in creating a better nation for us all.

(MORALITY/ETHICS) – Our Ancestors studied Creation in order to discover the nature of the order in themselves. They logically concluded that there is no possible better model than the Universe upon which to base and measure our humanity because it was the greatest thing in existence and it had forever worked as it should.

In the affairs of humans, they concluded that morality/ethics (the rules of what is right and wrong) is simple. Right is that which helps others and wrong is that which hurts them.

europeans are god-vyers. They believe that they are greater than the Creator and universal order. Either that or they believe that neither is real or not manipulable by them. So they have no choice but to be immoral and unethical because they operate outside universal order.

Oppression, exploitation, genocide, enslavement (as distinct from traditional Afrikan servitude) have no moral/ethical base. There is nothing moral/ethical about them. They are simply controlled chaos. Their closeness to the european, arab and asian heart and soul speak to how they define and play with morality and ethics to suit their own inhumane interests.

This is not the way of Afrikan people. We believe in divine order and work to order our minds, houses and nation accordingly. In dealing with other Afrikans, nationalists must always bear this in mind.

(SPORTS/ENTERTAINMENT) – Sports are supposed to improve one's athletic abilities, physical prowess and health. Entertainment is supposed to release the day's stress and make people reconsider their behavior and attitude toward each other. But, for the most part, that is not the purpose they serve in western society.

Given our belief in the european's superiority and disorder, not surprisingly, those we honor as being the most successful among us are no more than well paid slaves. They serve to entertain yurugu and increase their profits. And, given our general level of mentacide, it is not surprising that the majority of us who watch these activities

58

have become so vicariously lost in that fantasy that all of their (spare) time is consumed by them.

Afrikan nationalists do not have this time to waste on the distractions of seasonal sports and comedy, porno or whatever form the entertainment of those basking in their mentacide may take. We know that life is short, our nationbuilding problems are pressing and that three hours watching a game is better spent apprenticing our warriors-in-training.

This does not mean that we do not watch or engage in sports or take the time to rest and be entertained tastefully. It just means that we know the distractive, exploitative purpose of sports and entertainment for Afrikans in this cultural wasteland and we refuse to be distracted from our work or be exploited by enemies.

(MUSIC) – Warriors love music. Afrikans have always found themselves in the beat, the rhythm of the Universe, the Creator's heartbeat.

However, this place is not an Afrikan reality. The music flooding our community is designed to numb our senses to everything but baser physical and material appetites. So, we have to be very selective in what we listen to because we know that what goes in the ears influences the mind. And, because we know this, warriors think about the consequences of the music they select. We listen to music that is revolutionary/uplifting and which speaks directly to the spirit of our battles, loves and lives.

(ATTIRE) – As will be discussed further in "The Warrior's Appearance" chapter, we wear our consciousness. What people wear directly reflects who they are and their interests. No matter how we look at it, or how it has been twisted to make us want to give our money away so that we can look "hip" or "cool," image is everything in the west. We cannot get around appearance and the impression it gives to others of who we are, what class or position we hold in society and whose politics and vision we represent.

Therefore, as Afrikan nationalists, we have to be very deliberate and careful of the image we give to others through what we wear. Of course, our only concern over image is with those who are watching out of an earnest desire to also become powerful warriors. It is only for them and each other that we must diligently work to insure that the image we project is directly reflected in what we think, say and do.

(ELDER REVERENCE) – We do not worship our Elders. We honor them for who they are and what they have sacrificed to build for us. They deserve our utmost respect because they have diligently kept the path clear and faithfully carried the torch that lights our way long enough for us to take it so that we can see what lies ahead.

These are our Elders, not our olders. Olders are those mentacidal individuals who have done no more than grown old in our neighborhoods. They have consciously worked to subvert the nationalist path either by direct action or an inactive apathy or contempt.

Elders have always been there for us. They have lived and will die for us. There is no greater sacrifice one can give to Afrikan nationalism and we owe them beyond measure.

(ANCESTORS) – We honor no Ancestors other than our own. And these individuals came to be Ancestors because we see and remember them based on their lifelong record of service to family, community and nation. They are Ancestors because they have earned the right to be eternally honored in this way. We remember them through daily libations and by doing all in our power to walk in their footsteps so that we will eventually become one with them.

Those born of Afrikan blood who live lives unworthy of the respect of the warrior community are forever dismissed upon their deaths. We have no reason to clutter our lineage with the compromise brought by enemies within, dead or alive.

(SPIRITUALITY) – Black nationalists are deeply connected to our spiritual base. We know that spirit is the foundation and essence of all existence. We know that spirit is the source of our power. So, we place a great emphasis on the appreciation and cultivation of our higher selves.

Because the traditions of our Ancestors are known to us, we choose spirituality over religion. We are not controlled by manmade religious institutions and tolerate no religious persons who work through the religions others use against us. We submit to Spirit alone.

We easily obey the order, balance and peace offered by our higher minds. We control our material and physical appetites because we know that this self-restraint spiritually disciplines us.

(LEADERSHIP) – Every Afrikan nationalist is a leader. Each of us is watched and listened to, not just by enemies but by those who are beginning to question the logic of the chaos about them and are looking for models of power to emulate. Some of us are publicly known while others are not. But all of us are leaders, whether we recognize ourselves in this way or not.

As models of leadership, we should already have, or have begun to develop, the ability to both give and take instruction. Any leader worth following is humble. And humility requires that we be receptive to instruction from others.

Those unable to do so, or are only able to listen to instruction from enemies, are not leaders. They are misleaders. They show us the way into further captivity.

As Afrikans, we have to return to a model of leadership that emphasizes family. As representatives of a family centered nationalist movement, we have to move away from the desire to be individual "heroes" and "sheroes" to that of being one of two individuals forming a powerful complementary leadership. We have to return to a model of leadership where private and public life are not contradictory, where men and women have equal decision-making power (even if in different areas) and where two minds are understood to be more powerful than one.

This is fair. This is progressive. This is Sankofan. This follows the path of our Ancestors.

(COMMITMENT) – Afrikan nationalists have an unqualified, absolute commitment to the liberation, empowerment and sovereignty of Afrikan people. And we ever remain uncompromised and incorruptible by enemies within our community and those behind enemy lines. We seek guidance only from our Ancestors and the vision they have bestowed on us by virtue of their greatness. Therein lies our power.

We know we are righteous. We know we are winning. We see through the weakness of other peoples' power. We do not side with them in order to make our destruction easier to bear. We are committed to their destruction.

(DRUGS & ALCOHOL) – Warriors have *self*-respect. We do not sabotage our ability to master our own self-discipline through ingesting weakening, mind-altering substances. We are not escapists, walking around in an irresponsible stupor, seeking an artificial distance from that which ails us and/or our people through temporary flights to cloud nine. It is not our way to walk around intoxicated out of our right minds because our vision for our people and peace for ourselves have not come to pass according to our wishful time schedule. Drugs and alcohol are not substitutes for applying our righteous rage so effectively that these ailments will be removed as destructive forces in our communities and nation.

It is no secret that alcohol (and other drugs) do more damage than just to the individual consuming it. Drunken/high escapes from reality have a negative, ripple impact on everyone in the physical and social vicinity. For one thing, anyone who has been around someone who abuses alcohol knows the truth of alcohol's reputation for inciting a "hot" anger. It makes easy an anger that is completely unfocused and dangerously destructive to any and everyone present.

This lack of self-control, no matter how temporary, is totally uncharacteristic of warriors. Our energy must always remain cooly concentrated on frontline activities that build stronger relationships between Afrikan people, not cripple or destroy them.

(GOSSIP) – Warriors do not speak about that which

we do not *know*. We do not gossip about friends or enemies. Doing either blurs the vision and creates obstacles and issues where they do not exist. Before regarding any statement as truth we seek out its source to verify or dismiss it.

(SEXUAL ORIENTATION & ATTITUDE) – For Afrikans, this really should not even be a point of discussion. We are heterosexual, pure and simple. We do not engage in any form of white sex, including oral sex, anal sex, homosexuality, bestiality, pedophilia, threesomes, etc., as well as bisexuality and transgenderism. Our Ancestors were not sexual degenerates and neither are we.

Afrikan nationalists have a positive, procreative attitude toward consensual heterosexual sex. We do not see those of the complementary sex as (past or future) conquests. We do not see it as something to be counted because one's power and/or self-esteem cannot be measured by the number of individuals we have successfully taken to bed, i.e., conquered. The nationbuilder's mind is not constantly on the hunt for the physical versus a higher mental and spiritual ground.

And we do not see sexual intercourse as an arena. It is not a game where we play with people's heads and bodies. It is not an activity where we vent our frustrations with the world against the complementary sex. We do not abuse those we lay with.

We see sex as serving a procreative and bonding function between two mature, consenting adults. Sex is sacred. It is a sharing of procreative energy. It is something that should be experienced by committed complements.

It only becomes something to play with in the hands

of predators whose lives/minds are so twisted that they feel a pressing need to inflict their pain and insecurities on others.

(LEVEL OF SERIOUSNESS & SOCIABILITY) – To outsiders, Afrikan nationalists are thought to be too serious, too Afrikan, too Black, too revolutionary (as if any of these are possible for individuals conscious of the assault against their people). Many also see our steadfast refusal to forgive and forget, to just let it go, as a hindrance to letting life in.

Those who know us know better. We thoroughly enjoy life and, especially, those of like mind whose company we keep. We get along exceptionally well with those who, whether they agree with it or not, are respectful of what we do. It is those who are disrespectful, who want to lower us to their mentacidal level or simply destroy us, with whom we have no interest in being sociable.

In general, though, Afrikan nationalists focus their sociability on nationbuilding. Such individuals know that life is not supposed to be a constant party/playtime. Our situation necessarily calls for a more serious social life.

Warriors need to understand that it is the enemy's job to make play appear so much more attractive than work. And we have to recognize that most of these attempts to sabotage our concentrated, uncompromising focus come from confused individuals whose opinions matter to us.

In this effort to nullify serious Warriors and glorify Afrikans who want to do nothing more than play, they have been quite successful. In the same way that some would-be Warriors think that the revolution is an online chat, quite a few of yurugu's victims believe their play is actually work.

Play is primarily the activity of children. It allows

65

them to safely pretend to be something they are not. It allows them to live in a world of make believe where they can test their skills and practice the art of being an adult.

So, if nothing else, we have to be careful of the nature and amount of our "play" as adults. Knowing why, in the simplest of terms, is vital. If the children are our future, then what does what they see the "adults" around them doing tell them about what they should be like when they grow up? And what does it tell us about what the future holds for Afrikan people?

Ptahhotep, one of the most profound thinkers in ancient Kemetic civilization, said, "He who teaches speaks to the future." What are we speaking into existence? How are we defining the destiny of Afrikan children through what we say and how we act around them?

Aspiring Afrikan nationalists must decide how serious they need their lives to be. It is a question of integrity and survival. Do we want to focus our righteous rage into something constructive enough to create a reality where we no longer have to walk around constantly enraged or do we want to force ourselves to forget our ongoing destruction by spending so much of our time in play that we become more skilled than negroes at pretending that it is not happening?

At this point, some may be asking if being serious means that we cannot play. It absolutely does not. Warriors need to allocate time for relaxation, to enjoy our complements, our children and the other members of our community. We need to do this for many reasons, especially to ease the stress/tension that naturally occurs with warrioring.

In the end, the problem for Afrikan nationalists is not with recognizing the need for greater seriousness. It is with the difficulty of separating work from play and consistently being able to prioritize work over play.

So, being serious is just a matter of us becoming mature enough to distinguish between when it is time to play and when it is time to work. We have to be wise enough to know that when it is time to work we do not have time to play.

(RACE CONSCIOUSNESS) – Afrikan nationalists consciously, wholeheartedly, uncompromisingly believe in the doctrine of "Race First." Nothing in our political thinking overrides race as what we first and foremost identify with in this world. Race is our primary self-definition and the framework out of which we define reality. We understand that race and culture are socially, culturally, politically and genetically inseparable scientifically.

(POLITICS) – Afrikan nationalists are nationbuilders of the first order. We only work with like-minded builders. Alliances with enemies are the last thing on our agenda because we know that alliances create obligations and obligations with proven or potential enemies end in undesirable compromises.

We do not subscribe to electoral politics. Voting is for those who do not act and/or who believe that the european's corrupt social order is correctable. We have studied them and considered the possibilities of this corrupt order.

We define politics as the grassroots organization of our community around the interests that specifically serve us. We recognize only those who have been selected by the community as our leaders. It is a selection strictly based on

67

their record of service and loyalty to us. And we accept it as our personal responsibility to hold these appointed individuals accountable for their every single word and action.

The Warrior's Attitude

I will stay true to myself
I will always be loyal to those that's loyal to me
I will always demand respect and give respect

Stic Man & Young Noble

The Afrikan nationalist's attitude toward self and others in the community who see us as a people is one of the utmost respect. We do not judge ourselves as better or less than those we know and associate with in a nationbuilding way. We recognize that each of us has different abilities and levels of development as well as challenges and faults. Moreover, we understand that the assault against us makes us a little edgy and less trusting than we would normally be toward each other under ideal Afrikan conditions.

So, it is with humility, not arrogance, that we see and deal with each other. We approach each other with unqualified love, respect and understanding. We treat each other as best we can as the Brothers and Sisters that we naturally are. We do not allow what is going on outside our circles to cause us to be resentful, callous, indifferent, distant or uncivil/irreverent toward fellow Afrikan nationalists.

We are an army of warriors and warriors, like everyone else, have differences. But those differences should never place us at odds with each other because those "odds" will be used against us by our enemies.

The Afrikan nationalist's attitude toward enemies within and outside the community is quite the opposite. Except in actual combat, our response toward them should not be designed to reveal our true intent or activities. It must be one of deliberate caution because we are constantly aware that these interactions are with enemies or, at minimum, severely confused, disloyal individuals.

Therefore, it is in our best interest, and that of our nation, to keep enemies as far away as possible from what we know. They have no need to know. Furthermore, the historical record shows that no european, no negro, no lost soul, is to be trusted with the ideas or operation of our liberation movement. Those who will not directly use this against us are likely to confide our secrets to those who will.

Whether the distance we keep from enemies is one maintained through avoidance, silence or simply being politically noncommittal, it is one of our greatest shields against being infiltrated and corrupted from outside. We must always remain aware that we are building from within enemy territory. And we certainly must remember that their hunt for us never ceases, for they daily live with the terror of our awakening and their fall.

The Warrior's Appearance

Soldier for the struggle, yeah I gotta keep it crystal clear,
tighten up my belt so you can't see my underwear

Watoto from the Nile

We live in a society where the physical rules our minds. What you look like, your appearance and attire and the things you possess, exercise more influence over your chances in life than anything else. This is true regardless of where you live or what you do for a living. The quality of your character, the integrity and righteousness of your mind, heart and soul, lags far behind these in social value.

In fact, most of us act as if physical appearance and material worth are the only valid basis upon which we should judge each other. However, those of us aspiring to ancestral heights, those of us who truly know what it means to be a nationalist, know better. Minds of this caliber do not judge each other or other Afrikans so shallowly.

We know western society. We know its materialistic, image-based imperatives and priorities. We are clear that they are wrong, very wrong. We recognize that the mental is vastly more important than the physical. Of the significance of our spiritual base, we should be even more sure. Even if we have not yet given much thought to the connection between what people have and the material measurement of their worth in western society, it should be apparent in complaints we constantly hear from people about not being respected for their minds.

Peer groups are often the greatest culprits in this grand deception. Especially for those who feel powerless, peer groups are known for pressuring their members into dumbing themselves down. Unfortunately, this social manipulation is not just limited to the youth.

The objective is to reduce those needy enough to embrace a follower role to their most easily controlled state. Particularly among those of warrior class age, conspicuous consumption (i.e., buying to show off whatever is most popular and expensive) and being as sexually revealing, available and exploiting or exploited as possible are the common levelers.

Many of us are aware of the backwardness of this priority on appearance. But we still act as if we have no choice but to submit to a life limited by a physical matrix. It is as if we have lost our minds to things and can see no value beyond them. Many even try to rationalize this with the "when in rome do what the romans do" excuse. Weak but catchy phrases like this allow us to comfortably continue playing along with the game of focusing our attention solely on what we and others appear to be.

Though this submission generally applies to members of western society, it is especially the case for Black folk. Among a people who feels powerless, the drive to be seen reflects their belief that they have little of worth within. Because they mistakenly believe they are powerless and that power is only held by those they are allowing to rule them, they see little value in themselves. And, in a materialistic world, they are constantly driven to search for *things* outside of themselves to prove to themselves and others that they are worthy of existing.

Their unspoken, unconscious desire to be powerful is fulfilled by the things those they believe have power are willing to sell them. They believe that the power of the seller lies in those things.

Living in this grand self-deception, they have come to believe that what they look like and own and lease or rent are the most important indicators of their shallow identities. Those falling most for this are the weakest minded of individuals.

The degree to which many of them expose their bodies to the scrutiny of any and everybody indicates as much. Our bodies are our most personal quality and, therefore, should be our most private one. No one, except our complements (and/or physicians) should be able to see all of us. So, it is a major statement about our self-esteem when we publicly display what only those closest to us should be able to see.

People emphasize that which they feel are their best and most worthy qualities. And doing so tells others what they consider to be their most valuable assets. Weak people emphasize their bodies. Powerful people emphasize their minds.

We are not saying that the physical is irrelevant to our existence or definition of self. Saying that would be ignorant and irresponsible. Without the physical we cannot exist as human beings. We could not walk, talk, eat, build, attract and embrace each other, or reproduce ourselves. We would not exist in this physical reality.

But, to overemphasize the physical fits an enemy's plan for the misuse of our genius. It conforms to the european's hyper-sexualized priority. To act as if bodies and sexual play are the basis of life and living, and to do this at the expense of our mental, emotional and spiritual development as human beings, is to deny the significance of the vital thinking, feeling and divine part of our being.

In their present state of mind, Afrikans lost in western materialism belong to our enemies. In one way or the other, they spend all of their time, energy and resources studying, purchasing and wishing for empty consumer goods. They are dying to be seen.

For those Afrikans who want nationalism, for those of us who want to regain our self-respect, who want to belong to the Afrikan nation only, this focus on possessing meaningless trinkets must change. If all we are to each other is merchandise to be bought and sold, manipulated by the highest bidder, then we will never be more than commodities in someone else's market because we do not control that market and are only very minor players in it. We would remain slaves.

If we are to return to power, we must change our priorities. We must elevate above the material and physical when assessing ourselves and each other. We must raise the bar. We must emphasize our higher consciousness over our lower minds.

Sisters

Just as there is a difference between a woman and a girl, there is a distinct difference between Sisters who are nationalists and those who are not. There is an evident reverence for self within those Afrikan women who are nationalists, which is reflected in how they walk, sit and stand, what they say and how they say it, where they go and how they act there, the men they choose to be with, what they are willing to allow these men to do with them and how they expect these men to act toward them, publicly and privately. The same can be said of women-in-training, though their associations with men differ.

Certainly our Sisters are physically beautiful. This gift cannot, and should not, be hidden. But not recognizing their own natural inner beauty has led far too many of them to believe that they must sell themselves physically in order to be worthy in the eyes of those we can only call "adult" or "grown" males.

In addressing this issue, we have to be careful with assigning fault. These insecure Sisters are only part of the problem. Adult males make up the rest of it. If we do not consider the fact that like attracts like, we can end up looking in the wrong direction for the cause of this weakness or accepting only a partial reasoning as the whole story.

The adult males we are referring to are individuals who are legally of adult age but who do not qualify for manhood because they lack the intelligence, inner strength (personal sense of security and self-esteem), courage, psychological and emotional maturity and material independence to claim this honor. Their personal sense of security and self-esteem is absent or underdeveloped. Relative to their adult age, they are immature and even infantile. They are simply little boys in men's bodies.

Men, whose intelligence and maturity match or even surpass their adult age, automatically recognize our Sisters' external beauty for what it is — natural and incomparable. They spend the bulk of their time and energy pursuing the beauty and essence that can only be found within the heart, mind and spirit of a woman. Obviously, they have no interest in "adult females."

Only in those things which cannot be physically touched can a man find the essence of a woman. He knows that the physical is merely a reflection of that divine quality.

On the other hand, an adult male has never been able to rise beyond his uncontrollable appetite for pleasure. He has never known the real happiness a woman can bring in a relationship based on mutual respect. He does not have the maturity to get beyond the surface.

Operating at the lowest possible existence, his "love" is a purely physical experience. For him, "any love" will do. Sexual conquests define him. Physical, verbal and emotional domination of others is the only meaningful measure of the "manhood" he so desperately craves but cannot master because of his ignorance of self.

Sisters must not lower themselves to this walking insult to Afrikan womanhood. They must regard their bodies and appearance as sacred. And how they present themselves to the mirror and world should *always* reflect this divinity. Since we are here for each other, since we belong to each other, since we reflect each other, since there are no women without men (and vice versa), Sisters should always dress for Afrikan men, not the adult males who litter the "conscious" landscape.

A woman cannot act like a girl and expect a woman's respect from men. We should know that boys, whatever their age, will act like boys around females, whatever their age. In the same way, we should know that men will act like men around women (and fathers around girls).

The same applies for the mentality of females. Girls, whatever their age, will act like girls around boys and men. But women will act like women around men (and mothers around boys). There should be no other expectation.

The norm of females dressing as if their lives center around getting a man, any man, by showing as much of their bodies as possible, says a great deal about how little they think of themselves. Again, we display those qualities which we believe best reflect us. We emphasize and show off what we believe is most important about ourselves. We present to the public, and especially the individuals we would like to attract, our qualities of which we are the most proud and by which we most want to be judged.

We do this at a conscious and subconscious level. The conscious level can be easily seen in how we physically, mentally and socially present ourselves to the world. The subconscious level, which drives the conscious one, is also reflected in how we present ourselves but, more importantly, it tells the world *why* we present ourselves in this way. It indicates the level of respect and self-esteem we have for ourselves.

When everything centers on the physical and material, we are of no personal value to others, except through being used and abused. When we live to put on a show designed to gain that shallow, lustful, worthless attention so common in our community today, the message we send to those whom we should want and really need in our lives, those who would truly love us for who we are and help us to discover and strengthen our power within, is one of foolish rejection. It speaks volumes about our personal weakness, general lack of intelligence, insecurity and neediness, directionless emptiness (an unfulfilled, undefined, unloved self), absence of sound moral judgment and a virtual or complete absence of spiritual connection within

77

our lives. Moreover, it tells others that this is where we want to stay. It says we are comfortable in our self-denial and the limits others have imposed on us.

Therefore, because the Afrikan nationalist woman is a Queen, the Elder Mamas say she should dress appropriately. She should wear feminine clothing that is modest. She should not dress to look "sexy." Black women are naturally alluring.

As a woman of power, humility and quality, she knows when she has stepped over the line of decency. Her underwear should not be seen above, below or through her clothes. She does not put her breasts or thighs on display. People will not be able to see the crack of her behind or her midriff. She should not be seen in Daisy Dukes, miniskirts, low cut tops, leggings without an appropriate long top or dress, high splits, low rider pants or very sheer clothing. Sexy clothing should be reserved for the bedroom. She absolutely should not wear men's and/or masculine-looking. Decency dictates her attire and appearance no matter where she is or what she is doing.

Comfort is key. Her clothes should not be tight fitting. They should be loose enough to allow her skin to breathe and give her ample ease of movement. If she chooses to wear pants they, too, should be loose fitting and feminine, not constraining or conforming to the sex-focused eurocentric definition of sexy. And her shoes will not make her unbalanced and/or cause back issues, corns and bunions as she gracefully ages. They should not be very high heeled or stiletto. They should feel comfortable keeping her close to Mother Earth and allow her to run when necessary.

Her physical appearance also should not reflect an alien, unAfrikan definition of beauty. It is not artificial, unrealistic or undesirable. She does not allow others to exploit her through the purchase of wigs, weaves, extensions and/or unnatural colored hair dyes. Her hair is natural – soft, kinky, beautiful. Her skin and nails, too, are as the Creator gave them to her in all their genuine beauty. Make-up, if desired, is minimally applied to accentuate her Afrikan features, not hide them under a mask.

This is not to say that she should not adorn herself. That is always a woman's prerogative. But, when doing so, what is foremost in the Afrikan nationalist Queen's mind is modesty and decency. Some Sisters already understand this, so they easily operate at this genuinely original, high level of self-respect.

Unfortunately, others are still battling the subconscious imperatives of the sexist "meat market." The emptiness western socialization automatically breeds in them creates a neediness which diminishes their value. It causes them to do what would normally be considered unreasonable if the goal is to attract someone of worth. They endure lives of sadness, alone inside themselves. What they have been made into only attracts boys and adult males who only have the capacity to bring them a momentary true happiness.

However, thankfully, there are some Sisters who know the kind of company that being on sexual display brings and want no part of it. These women warriors already know that something is horribly wrong with how this reality would have them present themselves to the world. So, naturally, they look to the original, uncorrupted Afrikan woman as their guide for being themselves.

Nonetheless, mentacide dies slowly. Therefore, Sisters who are new on the Afrikan path need to know that we are all at various stages of personal development, so they should never torture themselves if they have not yet perfected their nationalist model of womanhood. Moreover, anyone who pretends to be perfect is either ignorant or an arrogant fool.

There are three final points which our Sisters should consider in relation to their search for an Afrikan nationalist complement of quality.

Firstly, you should not feel compelled to demean themselves in order to attract a man based on a male/female ratio imbalance. Quality, not quantity, is the critical variable.

Secondly, do not believe that you can change a boy into a man. Think about what you are attracting. Remember, what you did to get him you'll have to continue doing in order to keep him. This includes everything from interests to dress to sex to politics. And, if this means being his mother, you will have to hold his hand and walk in her shoes as long as you are able to tolerate him.

And thirdly, given that all Afrikan males have the potential to be powerful men, do not look at his potential and expect to be able to nurture his manhood in line with your politics. In other words, once you have won his affections, do not expect to be able to control him and, in this way, politically direct the expression of his potential.

This would be an act of deceit and will not turn out well. He will lose himself in the process and will consequently become increasingly resentful. Sadly, there are too many tragic examples of what this has done to long-term relationships in the nationalist community.

Brothers

Brothers whose minds have risen no higher than

their appearance are no better than their female counterparts. The worst of this group is those Black males who walk around in kilts or skinny jeans, who are saggin their pants, flaunting layers of rainbowed or cartooned underwear and their butt-cracks to other males. These are those males who line up to slip into whatever the next demasculinizing style that comes along. What they wear and how they wear it speaks volumes about their limited or nonexistent consciousness.

When Afrikan males dress like fags or effeminized males or cross-dress, they are exactly what they appear to be. But, what are they appearing to be? Psychologically, just what are fags, effeminized males and male cross-dressers?

In comparison to what Afrikan men (and men-in-training) should be and what we need on the frontline, they are no longer men. They represent the broken, mentally (and often physically) emasculated, impotent, weak, delicate, degenerate male our enemies need us to be in order for them to have unrestricted access to our women, children and every other valuable resource. They have become the truly vanquished, those who believe we have already lost this genocidal war against Afrikan people and want nothing more than to hide behind or under the skirts of their masters. They have no meaningful purpose in life other than possibly servicing yurugu when kneeling in front of his crotch or bent over his bed.

Once this has happened though, once a (potential) Black man has been reduced to the mind and/or image of a little white girl, yurugu have accomplished their principal goal of breaking that Afrikan's spirit. Consequently, they no longer have to fear him rising from the physical, mental and spiritual shackles they have custom designed for him.

Instead, he will do all in his power to find or make a way to your bedroom.

The public perception of Brothers when they dress as they believe thugs do is only different from this in degree. In the eyes of those who know, they look like punks and clowns. As the Brothers of United Front so poignantly say on their cut "Message to the So-Called Gangstas,"

...and ya'll supposed to be our soldiers, big, hardcore ganstas –
where you at?
when these crackkkas is killing us man.
now they killing our babies man.
where you at?
ya'll ain't doin' nothin', ya'll nowhere to be found.
ya'll ain't hard core. you ain't hard. you soft.

Those who put on this act to impress Sisters should grow up because they want warriors, not thugs (real or imagined).

We have to stop being so gentle in our criticism of and challenges to those who claim to be so hard. For, if they are as hard as they would have us believe, then they should be able to constructively take what we knowingly say. If they were truly that hard, they would be running this reality, not just feeding off of its crumbs; they would not be running from equally armed opponents; they would be preying on our enemies and not each other and innocent bystanders.

Unlike the so-called thugs, nationalist Brothers have to consider their primary role of securing the perimeter in how they dress. This is not a casual role. It is a deadly serious military one. Therefore, clothes and accessories, especially jewelry, must be evaluated in this light. *Everything* we put on must be judged based upon its utility as to its offensive and/or defensive applicability.

In terms of saggin', common sense should tell us that you need two hands to be effective in battle. How can you effectively fight, or quickly retreat, if one of your hands is occupied with holding your pants up? It is no wonder so many of our sons are so easily caught when running from agents of the state.

Not only do oversized, drooping pants pose difficulty for hand to hand combat because they will not stay up but, in general, baggy clothes are easier to grab, giving a tactical advantage to enemies in pursuit or in a wrestling match. Yes, loose clothing makes it easier to carry and conceal weapons but, at the same time, it automatically alerts others to the possibility that something is being concealed. For warriors, in most battle situations, less is more.

Fortunately, baggy clothes are not needed to conceal weapons. At minimum every warrior needs a pocket knife. It is a basic necessity for many reasons. Daily, knives can make cutting, opening and cleaning tasks easier. In worst case scenarios, they serve as defensive weapons, instruments of escape and tools for making other tools and other weapons. Needless to say, while carrying a pocket knife is desirable, having a concealed firearm (with a permit) is invaluable. In either case, we need to remember that carrying weapons into restricted areas can lead to confiscated weapons, fines and arrests.

A final point is directly related to the specific messages our clothes bear. This is a point which applies to the Brothers and Sisters equally. In terms of images, T-shirts and sweatshirts are of special concern because of the faces and symbols which decorate them.

As we indicated earlier in the book, it's important for Afrikan nationalists to take sides. If we are to earn respect, we have to take uncompromising moral and racial sides when thinking about living revolutionaries and those who have moved on to the ancestral realm. There have to be parameters, boundaries, absolutes that distinguish Afrikan nationalists from those pretending to be revolutionaries. And the most fundamental of these parameters is the unqualified philosophy of "No europeans, no negroes, no homosexuals (or "promos" – those who pretend not to be homosexual but defend the homosexualization of Afrikans even more fiercely than those who are openly homosexual)."

To this end, we should not be wearing clothes having the faces of the likes of Angela Davis, James Baldwin, Alice Walker, Maya Angelou or C.L.R. James on them. Angela Davis is dedicated to the homosexualization of Afrikan people (publicly promoting gender confusion in its various forms) and a marxist. In spite of his racial insight and literary genius, James Baldwin was a devout homosexual. Alice Walker is an interracialist who married the enemy and is unequivocally pro-homosexual. One has to wonder exactly what kind of whitened future Maya Angelou would direct our attention to when she wrote "still I rise," given that two of her marriages were to europeans. And C.L.R. James was also married to a european. Moreover, he was a devout marxist who led the negro movement within the communist/socialist party to destroy Marcus Garvey and the UNIA. A person's character must consistently reflect his or her public statements if he or she is to be taken seriously by Warriors, so always know whose image you have on display.

There are plenty of Afrikans who fill the requirements of Afrikan nationalism whose faces should be displayed for their loyalty to The Race. If an Afrikan nationalist is to wear a T-shirt or sweatshirt featuring a face, it should be the image of Nat Turner, John Henrik Clarke, Amy Jacques Garvey, Harriet Tubman, Nana Kuntu (Del Jones), Hannibal Afrik, Amos N. Wilson, Ida B. Wells or the like. These, and only Afrikan nationalists like these, are the faces that should be honored with a place on our clothing and the walls in our homes.

To be clear: No one's trying to tell you what to wear. Only fools or megalomaniacs would truly believe they have the power to decide that for others. Instead, you are being asked to think about how you want to be seen, what powerful imagery you want to share and what message you want to send.

Those who claim to be nationalist must understand that there is a proper protocol, etiquette, way of dressing and behaving that is characteristic of nationbuilding warriors. There is a correct way to be and reflect a privilege that, at this time in ourstory, only a few deserve.

In society, everything is political. And, since this is so, our clothes need to be a revolutionary political statement. They need to convey an Afrikan nationalist message to all within eyesight. There are those who may think otherwise, but you cannot avoid the fact of the impact of your appearance. You cannot not make a statement.

What you wear says something. It tells the world the kind of person you are, what you value, what your politics are, your level of intelligence and the vision you hold for yourself and your people. Knowing this, the only question you should be asking yourself is what is what you are wearing saying.

No one has the right to dictate to you what you wear. However, a wise warrior carefully considers what people think when they see him or her. They give serious thought to the question of whether or not potential Afrikan nationalists see a contradiction in what you say when looking at what you wear.

Whether we choose to adhere to it or not, we at least need to agree that there is or, at least, should be, an unspoken "Nationalist's Dress Code" that is based on elevating communalism and self-respect over individualistic materialism and self-hatred. It holds decency over impropriety and highlights the considerable difference between making oneself respectfully presentable and being dysfunctionally conspicuous.

As we close this discussion about the Black nationalist's appearance, a couple of important points need to be mentioned. The first is about attitude. We must never forget the importance of giving and receiving sincere, deserved praise for being prominent models of well ordered, respectfully attired warriors.

So, do not give or take compliments lightly. And appreciate the honor felt for you behind those given from the heart. However, be wary of those given in excess. Most often, these words come from tongues which belong to envious persons. Undue, excessive flattery comes from those who want nothing better than to bring you down below their fearful, insecure, broken level.

The other point has already been made. And it is that our eternal military vigilance must be reflected in what we wear. There must be a conscious functionality in our attire. Readiness for battle dictates a certain practical type of attire, regardless of setting or occasion. Everything, our clothes, shoes, hairstyles, jewelry, accessories, everything must support our military mind.

What we choose to wear must go beyond our

personal preferences and find expression in our frontline needs. In the process, we must develop the ability to easily fuse our individual personalities and tastes with our collective nationalist activities in what we wear.

In conclusion, respect for self must be worn in order to be recognized and acknowledged by others. We have to pay close attention to what we, as representatives of the nation's frontline, put on. We should be seen and see each other positively. The respect we demand from this world must be taken through the power of our presence.

Respect is taken, not given, through one's character and presence. And it is not an individual phenomenon for nationalists. We represent an unfolding, returning nation. Therefore, we must always remember our unwritten code of decency.

Why do we say "unwritten?" Times change. Styles change. Traditional attire is rediscovered and marketed as new, often by the unconscious looking to exploit aspiring warriors with something Afrikan. We must be in the position to judge what makes Afrikan sense in whatever we wear whenever it appears. We must be in the frame of mind which allows us to individually judge each new piece of attire in terms of it fitting or failing our image of decency.

Regardless of who brings it or where it comes from, we must always bear in mind that this place and time is not ancient/traditional Afrika. Most often, the reason and meaning we gave to what we wore then cannot be fully understood or appreciated in whiteland.

How we dress and present ourselves has to reflect the highest qualities of self-respect for who we are as a people. We have to dress as members of a vanguard who place the highest value on their minds.

Being an Afrikan nationalist is not a choice. It is an ancestral obligation. And those who follow the only path which will liberate, empower and make Afrikan people sovereign have to provide the nationbuilding model. We have to set the highest possible standard of what it means to be an Afrikan woman or man.

And, yes, to do this we need to be our own moral police. We have to pay attention to each other, give serious thought to the constructive criticism we receive from each other and be on constant guard for each other. We should always be asking ourselves "what would our Elders and Ancestors think" about how we appear to each other and our people.

The Warrior's Words

[If] you're gon' be teachin' folks things, make sure you know what you're sayin'
Older folks in our neighborhood got plenty of know-how
Remember if it wasn't for them, you wouldn't be out here now
And I ain't comin' at you with no disrespect
All I'm sayin' is that you damn well got to be correct
Because if you're gonna be speakin' for a whole generation
And you know enough to try and handle their education
Be sure you know the real deal about past situations

Gil Scott Heron

Words are powerful. They are the means through which thoughts create reality. We create our world out of what we think. And what we think forms and guides what we say. In turn, words define our possibilities and dictate what we build.

Regardless of the pictures involved in our imaginings, we speak to ourselves in words. We think about and describe these imaginings in words. We think in words. Words and thought are inseparable.

However, since we cannot truly tell what people are thinking, we have to rely on what they say to see inside their minds. So words become the true (as far as we can tell) indicator of a person's sense of self-worth, perception of others, view of this or any other society and vision of what is/needs to come. At the level of interpersonal relationships, words are critical.

Easily, words (like thoughts) can build and destroy relationships and realities. At the personal and interpersonal levels, they can open or close minds to truths and possibilities unimaginable before they are introduced as ideas. They can magnify or shrink the good and/or bad individuals see in themselves and others. They have the ability to lift people up to the highest heights of happiness or drag them down into the deepest depths of despair. They can bring people together into an unbreakable, unified whole or fragment them into selfish, insecure parts always in hate with each other. Words are powerful beyond words.

Words are sounds. Sounds are vibrations. Our words are sounds formed by the vibrations of our vocal cords. The Universe, too, is vibration. And everything in it, the All, vibrates.

Because we are fundamentally, spiritually, a people of sound, because we are finely in tune with this rhythm, the vibration of the Universe, words (sounds created through vibration) resonate most deeply within us. When spoken, words flow on this rhythm. This is why the oral tradition, the communication of ideas primarily through verbal conversation, has naturally developed among us far beyond what it has in other racial groups.

We feel things in ways no other people can because we are more intensely connected to Spirit. We can recognize this in our music, in its vibration, in its beat. We could never do without the feel of the bass.

And, because of this spiritual trait, we are more keenly aware of others' energy and more intensely affected by it than others. We are a people of the soul. So, words and imagery damage or strengthen us in ways others are unable to imagine. This truth applies even for those of us who appear to have become disconnected from our true selves. We more than hear words. We feel them.

In traditional (normal) Afrikan society this connection is a gift. But this environment is neither then nor there. In this arrhythmic, anti-Afrikan reality, most of us can no longer appreciate the uniqueness and power of our rhythm. Most of us are no longer mentally in our original state and have no desire to return to our natural way of being. We have become willing captives to yurugu's despiritualized rhythmlessness. In yurugu's world words curse us because the enemy is controlling the language and directing the messages that come with the music we naturally make.

This submission to an existence of negative vibrations has taken some time to come about. It is because of who we are at the level of spirit that it has taken so long and so much violence to break us from our spirit. It has taken the harshest words and most barbaric deeds to force us to voluntarily lower ourselves into the bowels of this anti-Afrikan hell.

In babylon, our senses are assaulted in ways that our ancient Ancestors could never have anticipated for those who came after them. This is not the way of humanity. This is not human. It is not even the way of animals, for even "lower" life forms respect each other. Even if they kill one another for food or protection, it does not involve humiliation or torture.

It is the nature of our seemingly eternal confinement

in this particular hell that we have degenerated into what we see about us. We have become numb sponges to the negativity assaulting us. Many have even fallen for this negativity, promoting it and believing themselves to be the niggas and bitches they call each other. And, because racist oppression and exploitation has left us ignorant, powerless and, therefore, feeling that we deserve this self-hatred, we violently strike out against ourselves and each other with words because we can no longer see the source of this pain.

Knowing this and that nationalists are a different breed of Afrikan, what words should we use and not use when addressing each other and which ones should we not be using against each other? What should we call and not call ourselves?

First and foremost, Sisters should never be referred to as a bitches or ho's because they are neither, pure and simple. No elaborate explanation is required. That is just not what they are. By nature, Afrikan women are not canines. They are not animals roaming the streets in constant heat longing to be sexually ravished. Traditionally, they do not give away their bodies for money or for free to males who they do not know, or who they are not committed to and who are not committed to them.

They are our Queens, our most valuable resource. They nurture us, show us compassion and give us life. They are the essence of the feminine beauty we have carried throughout time. They are incomparable.

Similarly, brothers should never be referred to as niggas, dogs, pimps or playas because they are none of the above, pure and simple. No elaborate explanation is required.

They are our Kings, our providers and protectors. Their strength has always built what our genius demanded.

They are the epitome of masculine power on this Earth.

The list of derogatory terms, words that spew forth disgust with and hatred for ourselves, is endless. No doubt, it will continue to grow and worsen as long as we continue to see ourselves through the envious, fearful eyes of europeans. Some Afrikans will even use their misguided genius to manufacture theories or search for linguistic similarities that, in their warped, frustrated imaginations, somehow make these names ours. Those who are most desperate for "Afrikan" terms which fit or are the same as the epithets europeans have so long used to dehumanize us ignorantly identify with, promote and celebrate their use in an alien reality, a world far outside any Afrikan social, cultural context.

So, it serves no purpose to give a list of those words which identify us in the worst of all possible ways. We know what they are and will be able to follow any change in them. The few we have used here will suffice to prove the point.

The popular lie is that these hateful words are terms of endearment, praise names or ancient national identities. But they are not expressions of love for each other. And, even if they were, this is not then and, obviously, we are not, by a long shot, those Ancestors. Common sense should tell us this. But, similar to those who feel themselves drowning in a pool of water, people desperate to safely find themselves in someone else's nightmare, a nightmare to which they can see no reasonable escape, will grab onto anything to survive the slaughter.

Terms of endearment are supposed to mentally and emotionally bring us together. They should not divide us and call our men and women out of their names. Words like these are supposed to compliment us and express a sincere appreciation for our and each other's existence. They are supposed to indicate just how much we love and respect each other. They are supposed to be vibrations which we use to elevate one another and lead each of us to become and be our best.

A compliment to a Sister from a Brother is a compliment to the Brother because we are one. The same applies for compliments given by Sisters to Brothers, Sisters to Sisters and Brothers to Brothers. We belong to each other. We are one.

We should especially take note of this destructive, hurtful, contradictory language in relations between Sisters and Brothers. Sisters are our women and Brothers are our men. There is no denying that we are a direct reflection of each other and that the greatness and beauty of one reflects the greatness and beauty of the other, as does the weakness and ugliness.

No term that lowers the character or potential of the complementary sex should be expressed publicly or in private among Afrikan nationalists. Such thoughts should not even occur. We cannot build family through the negativity of hatred or fear. And just as we cannot love anyone else until we love self, we cannot love ourselves until we love each other. We are one and the same.

We are here to lift each other up together. There is no other path to our success as a nation.

Accordingly, Brothers should always refer to the women in our community as Sisters, Queens, Lionesses, Priestesses, Goddesses, Mamas or some similar compliment. Our women should see each other in the same way. And they should individually and collectively work to exemplify the highest of these compliments.

For the same reasons, Sisters should always speak to the men in our community as Brothers, Kings, Lions, Priests, Gods, Babas or some similar compliment. Our men should refer to each other likewise. And they should individually and collectively work to exemplify the highest of these compliments.

Of course, we are not on this planet by ourselves. So, a word or two on how we speak to and address enemies within and outside our community would be in order here.

We should always be cordial to other Afrikans, friend or foe, unless they are not cordial to us. And the level of cordiality we express should reflect the degree to which their self-hatred is turned against us. The more self-hatred they express toward us the less cordial we need to be toward them. No Afrikan nationalist should allow themselves to be disrespected in greetings or conversations with other Afrikan people, ever.

Most of us have the ability to remember when we were openly, ignorantly mentacidal. Our memory of this should keep us humble enough to not dismiss the possibility of others coming into consciousness. So we should exercise some degree of patience when dealing with those who do not know they are Afrikan but who have the capacity and willingness to learn.

Being upset with individuals because of their mentacide is like intentionally driving in the slow lane and getting upset because the driver in front of you will not speed up. At that moment, this is where they are most comfortable. And, whether we understand it or not, or like it or not, that lane is theirs at that time.

In these instances, take the time to remember what you were like before you woke up to our destruction.

Remember that warriors are healers. That's a given because we destroy what is hurting our people. We remove the sources of our pain.

We have to remember that there is always the possibility that they, too, may wake up. If so, they will need to have someone who is uncompromisingly conscious to approach without fear of being ignored or dismissed. It is our job to assist.

Nonetheless, again, how negroes and lost souls respond to us is how we should respond to them. As long as we know who they are and what their politics are, they cannot hurt or distract us through conversation. As long as we know that they operate, whether consciously or not, in the interests of enemies we should be wise enough not to engage them in conversation which will give them insight into our politics, memberships and activities we do.

On the other hand, europeans, arabs and asians fall outside the circle of those with whom Afrikan nationalists converse. There is no reason for conversation between them and us. There is no need to cordially smile at them, pick up something they dropped for them, hold doors for them, offer a seat on the bus to them (regardless of sex, race, age or deformity) or lie to them about how cute their baby is.

If we happen to feel any sense of pity or humanity toward them, their history and what they continue to do against Afrikan people should provide a quick reminder that "smiling faces tell lies." Afrikan nationalists are not historically naive or gullible. The smile of an enemy is the smile of an enemy. At the personal level, enemies should be invisible to us.

On the battlefield we see them clearly. And because the battlefield is everywhere, we should treat them accordingly everywhere. Only in situations where we have no choice, as when we are in their employ or in need of a service they offer which we cannot at this moment provide for ourselves, or where our ability to feed, clothe and heal (as in medical emergency situations) ourselves and our families, is communication with enemies appropriate. Still, even in these instances, what we say to them should be limited specifically to the issue at hand. Our task here is to keep them unknowing and off-guard.

The Warrior's Complement

Consciously creating life.
The quintessential element of revolution supreme.

Narubi Selah

Afrikan nationalists do not sleep with the enemy.
We are at war. There is no other logical, reasonable,
acceptable explanation for our situation and how we should
be interpreting it. Therefore, we have no love for enemies.
Indeed, those who sleep with the enemy commit treason
against their Ancestors, an unspeakable crime.

We do not date or marry anyone other than those
whose Ancestors are the same as ours. And only Afrikans
are Afrikans. Rape and invasion do not qualify any
european, arab or asian for membership or, especially,
ancestorship. Only we are Afrikan. We love and build
with Afrikans only, intimately and publicly.

Within The Race, we do not keep the company of
those misguided individuals who play and sleep with the
enemy. The invasive weaknesses of deeply mentacidal
individuals can only poison the warrior's spirit. Only those

who we want to influence us should be in our presence.

Possibly the most important rule for Afrikan nationalists as we maneuver our way through the sexual gauntlet of yurugu's insanity is that we do not engage in homosexual, bisexual, transgender or any other anti-heterosexual thought or behavior. We are not sexually insane, degenerate or perverse. As our Ancestors, we are strictly heterosexual.

And we should feel absolutely no need to qualify, explain or defend ourselves to anyone who does not have the will or capacity to understand the fundamental incorrectness of their mentacidal love for alien, dehumanized ways. Warriors only do that which is normal and natural for human beings.

Knowledge of this goes as far back as we do. According to the Oracles of Ma'at (which, by the way, was a late recording of the rules of our way), Afrikan nationalists do not engage in sodomy. In general, sodomy includes all forms of sexual perversion. Oral and anal dis-sexual behavior are included in this definition.

Like the Universe, we are procreationists. We build complementary relationships between men and women. We produce children whom we consciously rear into powerful, productive warriors who, upon maturity, will build warrior families. Together, we, as a timeless people, from one generation to the next, provide the foundation for continuously, progressively building ourselves into the nation we have always been. This is our agenda. This is our mission. This is our vision.

True Afrikan nationalism can only be understood and advanced in the context of family-building. At its center lies marriage and rearing warriors to be family-building Afrikan nationalists. Rearing nationalists is the primary responsibility and mission of the parents and adult community because there is absolutely no guarantee that the children of Afrikan nationalists will follow in their parents' footsteps. Rearing nationalists is something that must be consciously, actively done. It does not just happen because they are born to us.

Complementarity refers to the serious, obligatory, personal, intimate, primary loving relationship between an Afrikan man and an Afrikan woman. Hence, for Afrikan nationalists, complementary relationships must be based on mutual respect, a reciprocal selflessness and a genuine concern for and unqualified trust of each other. Most importantly, though, if the two are to survive as one formidable frontline force, there must be a common vision and political interpretation of reality. Based on the idea that we are beginning to form a relationship of commitment to the other person, and not purchasing another toy to play with, we have to take the universal imperative of complementarity most seriously.

Still, again, the primary goal of a nationalist man or woman is the formation of family. Their Creator-given priority is to have and rear children into worthy nationalists who will continue the process of dating, marriage and family building necessary for the re-establishment and survival of an Afrikan reality and world.

Do not think in short-sighted terms. Lose the need for instant gratification. It has no place on the frontline.

Afrikan nationalism is timeless. It is a never-ending, intergenerational construct and mandate. Being Afrikan and exclusively working with other Afrikans to build a better reality for our great, great, great, great grandchildren is an ideology, a personal philosophy, a way of thinking and viewing reality and effectively acting on that thought and view. If we are to survive and be Afrikan, it is a vision which must deliberately be passed on from one generation to the next. Therefore, instilling children with a family priority must be intentionally kept at the center of the most important institution we have for passing on what and who we are and want to become – the family. Afrikan nationalists are family first. Race first is a given.

Our attraction should be toward one individual of the opposite sex at a time. And, if complementary relationships dissolve, there should be ample space between one and the next to seriously reflect on what went wrong and the work we need to do on ourselves. There must be adequate time to intelligently and soberly identify exactly what we must change and who we are looking for in order to expect a more successful outcome the next time.

Elders can be consulted in these instances. Depending on your age set, few among our peers are as qualified to assist. Certainly, none have greater experience and wisdom. And, when they are allowed to guide us in making good complementary choices, who is better suited for assisting those younger than them in choosing a mate than those who love you and Afrikan people more than life itself?

We must be careful in our discussion of complementarity not to discount the special role of polygamy. Having more than one wife or husband has its place in our traditions. However, it was based on the individuals involved having the maturity to not see the set of relationships as an extended playground. And it required the primary individual to *already* have the established means to materially, physically and spiritually provide for all involved.

However, we still have to remember that this is not

traditional Afrikan society. And, for most Afrikans caught up in western society and imperatives, the maturity and means to handle this most serious of obligations is absent or limited. Still, for those who have the maturity, understanding and will to formally work with more than one complement in building family and nation, this could be an option. However, community/village approval and support are needed to assist these families be Afrikan.

The Warrior's Preparedness

What if u woke up in the morn
@ the crack of dawn
looked out the window and seen that it was on
would you be prepared
would yah family starve
what if they cut the water supply and all the food was gone....
think contingent
if you plannin on existin
What if em to death

United Front

    At the heart of every Afrikan nationalist's life lies the concern for securing our spaces against alien invasion. Above all else, it is a mandate that calls for us to ever be prepared for any threat, any incursion, any emergency. And the most important words here are "to ever be prepared," or what in military circles is called preparedness.

    As servants of our people who know our most primary job is to defend them, *we must never be caught unaware of or ill prepared for any threat,* no matter how small or insignificant it may seem. Every threat is a threat.

What this should mean to us as frontline warriors is that we are responsible for our community's security. Knowing this, security should be present anytime we are anywhere together. It should be second nature, everywhere and at all times. Further, knowing that practice makes perfect, we should *always* be focused on operating at our highest possible skill level when doing so.

Preparedness, which is the cornerstone of any efficient human security system, also requires much practice and proficiency. For this reason, we offer the following training and evaluation checklist for Black nationalists. Because security is subject to all kinds of conditions and situations, the range of skills warriors should be familiar with vary greatly. Our attitude toward this should be of what we would need to know to start from nothing and survive long enough to build a nation.

Every Afrikan nationalist, regardless of age, sex, resources or location, should put as much energy as possible in becoming as well qualified in each of these as they can so as to be prepared for *any* exigency/situation. Use the following checklist to gauge your own preparedness. Do not dismiss these skills as irrelevant or beyond your abilities. Learn as much as you can about each as you are able. Any level of experience can prove beneficial to us. Take the time to consider why each is important for our survival and the nationbuilding process.

Afrikan Nationalist's Skills Checklist

	Expert	Many	Some	Few	None
Martial Arts					
Archery					
Cooking					
Carpentry					

Car and Small Engine Mechanics				
Gardening				
Swimming				
Canning				
First Aid				
Fishing				
Sewing				
Plumbing				
Electrical Wiring				
Camping, Hiking & Backpacking				
Rifle, Gun & Shotgun Shooting				
Exercise & Fitness				
Canoeing/ Rowing				
Map & Celestial Reading				
Survival Training				
Gunsmithing				
Chemistry				
Engineering				
Masonry				

In a focused mind, the more skills the better. And every skill can be useful in war's arena.

In addition to being knowledgeable and/or proficient in these areas, a significant amount of attention also needs

107

to be paid to the design and execution of security drills. Specifically, security drills are for the purpose of positioning adults in alert, protective positions and making our children invisible to the enemy. Like the fire, tornado, hurricane, earthquake and flood drills we are already well familiar with, they are designed to save lives and, if possible, secure property and space.

Since the 1950s we, unlike other groups, have totally neglected our emergency security drills. We believe that we are "american" and that europeans have the equipment, manpower, knowledge, readiness and desire to secure us with them in times of danger. Most importantly though, we do not see them as a threat.

Interestingly, and though it should be common sense, security drills are the one aspect of communal security that we seriously overlook. However, their importance to our safety in the face of this terror we call western society can never be emphasized enough.

At this time, wherever we are on this planet, we are in alien occupied spaces. And nationalists should never feel secure in any space we do not fully control. Never. Therefore, we must take our security drills more seriously than any other type of survival strategy because the greatest threat to our existence comes from other people, not natural disasters.

So, what do the children do and what do the adults do when an alien threat comes to the front door? the back door? any given window? is able to successfully enter the premises? What plans have been put in place? What early warning systems have been established? What drills are regularly exercised which will alert and move us into planned, practiced action in defense of our children and space? If we truly believe that we are at war, then we should be acting accordingly.

Let common Afrikan sense be your guide as to what to do and how to do it. Who knows what, should always be determined on a need to know basis. What you do and how you do it, should not be part of any public discussion.

The Warrior's Action

Oh beautiful black minds
Create, create the world for children to play with life
And not with death

Last Poets

Why are so many of us always trying to find the easiest way out of the most dire and difficult situations? We have moved so far away from being the men and women our Ancestors were. We have forgotten the example and words of those in our lineage who demonstrated by example that struggle is good, that adversity reveals and builds character.

Even losing has its benefits because it teaches the lessons that lead to winning. There is wisdom gained through retreat. There are lessons in having to go back and regroup. When setback, our energies become more focused in preparation for the next battle when we take the time to study why we erred rather than focusing on the resulting error.

As long as we do not take retreat, regrouping and

making mistakes as outright defeat, we are winning. When this becomes clear, when we accept that victory is our *only* option, we can truly recognize that there are no losers among warriors. There are only learners on the way to mastery.

Fighting against our lower mind and others' treacherous tricknology builds inner strength by testing the current limits of our knowledge and abilities. Overcoming obstacles which may interfere with us being our best automatically moves us in the direction of being better than we have ever known.

Only through struggle, only in making the stand of an undefeatable warrior, only acting "as if it is impossible to fail," can we learn just how good we are at defeating enemies inside and outside ourselves. Our Ancestors understood the value of soul searching struggle for a warrior's physical, mental and spiritual development. We should, too.

Warriors who lose their will most often do not do so because they believe that the european is right and/or that race is irrelevant. They do so because their struggle appears to be a losing battle against the increasing number, and more publicly supported voice, of Afrikan folk who believe so.

What prevents some Afrikan nationalists from acting like the warriors they are is their questions about the community's willingness to support them once they take a stand. Given what has happened to so many of our dedicated warriors at the hands of agents of this government, this is a reasonable doubt.

However, this is an irrelevant obstacle. We do what needs to be done because it is righteous, not because it is safe. We answer to the community of our Ancestors and children. And we do this without any expectation of what they, in turn, will do for us.

Being a warrior is a selfless decision. We do not make this choice because it may make us rich and famous. We already are. The wealth and renown of the Afrikan warrior spirit that courses through our veins, invigorating, honing and freeing the nationalist's heart and soul, is incomparable and beyond measure.

So, it makes no difference who's got your back or is by your side. It makes no difference how many of the enemy or us there are at any given time or place we meet. If there are twenty thousand of them and one of you, it makes no difference. In fact, determined warriors would argue that these are very good odds. It simply means that there are so many of them that every blow will strike someone.

Even knowing that Afrikan nationalists are never alone, even knowing that we are a community, an army of warriors, the odds are irrelevant to those who act on righteousness. A warrior can stand alone.

We do what we do simply because it is right. And we do this because it is what we were brought here to do. We need no other reason.

Righteousness is a warrior's highest calling. And this calling lies far above group consensus. It is based on universal principles of what is right and wrong. Whatever is good and beneficial is right. That which is bad and hurtful is wrong.

So what possible excuse would lead any true Afrikan nationalist to believe that doing nothing about the destruction of his or her people is right simply because a majority of these confused victims believe it to be so? We have to be wise enough to know that white people could care less if they are right or wrong. What's most important to

113

them is controlling the minds and bodies of others and being defended as having the right to do so by those they trample all over.

The Ancestors sent us to do this work. If we were not able they would not have sent us. Besides, we should know that we are our Ancestors. Their courage then and our presence now should tell us that having knowledge and ability but doing nothing with them to help our people is treason. It is treason against our Ancestors because they are the roots that nourish every Afrikan person and treason against ourselves because we come and feed from those roots.

No other motivation outside righteousness should be necessary for us to think, speak and act as Afrikan nationalists. We are keenly aware that no one else among our people has the courage, determination or know-how to do this work. Of equal importance, we should know that no one outside our nation should feel they have the right to do it. This is our responsibility, and if others are allowed to do it for us, we will forever be in their debt.

One way or another, the gaining of freedom incurs a debt. Either we seize it for ourselves and the debt is to our children and their children and their children. Here, it is a debt to maintain that freedom. Or others "give" it to us and our debt is in the form of eternal gratitude, loyalty, submission and servitude to their assumed superiority. In this case, debt is slavery. Know that the value of liberation is determined by the intensity and self-sufficiency of the effort that those who want it put into it.

Measuring our effectiveness as Afrikan nationalists requires that we take a good hard look at the kind of work we do for a living. And though what we do to survive may

114

not be as well-known as our nationbuilding activities, the jobs we hold are also very critical to our self-definition.

What we do to earn our living should not contradict our work as nationalists. But if need dictates that it do so, there should be a concrete plan in place to eventually remove that contradiction through self-employment or employment in something more in line with our nationalist agenda.

Be that as it may, we are trying to answer the question of exactly what kind of jobs Afrikan nationalists hold. Of course, it would be unreasonable or impossible to list or dictate what kinds of employment warriors should have. We are individuals, with individually tailored collections of talents. Still, the point must be re-emphasized that Afrikan nationalists should not be engaged in occupational pursuits which contradict our nationalist agenda, i.e., jobs which work to assist others to further enslave Afrikan people.

To state this in the most instructive terms, the nation comes first. So, while the work nationalists choose to do will naturally be based on the talents and skills we were individually blessed with from birth, it is imperative that we have the humility to recognize that the type of work we actually do must, first and foremost, be based on what the nation needs. All work must be specifically directed toward the improvement of the condition of Afrikan people and our eventual return to sovereignty.

This is a non-negotiable imperative because nothing short of sovereignty, the complete self-government, self-determination, self-definition of Afrikan people by Afrikan people, will do. A vision of absolute sovereignty always and ultimately defines the Afrikan nationalist's actions in employment and otherwise.

Given the genocidal relationship we have with europeans and others, in the mind of Afrikan nationalists sovereignty automatically means the conscious physical, mental and spiritual separation of Afrikan people from all our enemies. Only in those instances where trade or negotiation are called for would this rule be temporarily suspended. And, of course, in those cases, only a small number of us would be involved and whoever they are dealing with would be fully aware that they speak for us and are backed by a powerful people who remember what has been done to us.

Sovereignty also has a special relationship to our treatment in the western *criminal* injustice system. And the nature of this "special relationship" dictates that we define sovereignty in a way that ends our being controlled, contained and abused by it. Therefore, for us, sovereignty would have to mean that only we will decide on one of our own's guilt; only we determine who will and will not be punished for a crime and what that punishment will be; only we give the final say on imprisonment or capital punishment for an Afrikan man, woman or child we find guilty of a crime against Afrikan people. No one else can be allowed to do this, especially through the elected, appointed or otherwise employed state agents who look like us.

Using Frances Cress Welsing's listing of the areas of people activity, we can easily tell the difference in thinking between sovereign and subject peoples.

	Afrikan nationalists	**negroes/ lost souls**	**europeans**
economics	invest in own community; wealth building focus	invest in others' communities; income-spending focus	exploit others to create investments in own community; focus on hoarding wealth
education	learning for liberation; intelligence focused; emphasis on thinking	credentials for a job; trivia focused; emphasis on memory	schooling to control others' access to jobs and wealth
entertainment	focus on edutainment	blind search for stardom; all-consuming desire to be "rich and famous"	use others to entertain them; focus on profiting from others' talents
labor	work for self; believe in their products	work for others; produce to consume; work to purchase what they produce for others	have others work to produce what they consume
law	fight for human rights (and civil rights) and sovereignty for Afrikan people	fight only for those civil rights which do not upset a white dominated status quo and allow for their	make laws as easily changeable tools/rules for controlling others

117

		subintegration	
politics	politics as people organized in self-interest; accountability of all participants critical	believe they are full participants in western "democracy"; voters without leaders' accountability	politics to control others' resources and loyalties
religion	spiritual; non-religion focused	religious; non-spiritual	religion as a political weapon
sex	sex for procreation and love	sex for play, ego gratification and acceptance	sex for pleasure and domination
war	fight for the liberation of Afrikan people	believe the european's wars against the world are about spreading democracy	use wars to conquer and steal; imperialist agenda/visio n

Now, let's take a closer look at these differences.

Economics

Afrikan nationalists know the importance of financially and materially investing in the physical, mental and spiritual foundation and well-being of their own community and people. We place our financial energy into strengthening the whole Afrikan nation through empowering all individuals involved. The end goal is self-sufficiency through the creation, investment and reinvestment of wealth in everything and everyone who builds national power. We understand that an economic order is more about how people see and relate to each other in terms of their providing for each other's needs than a simple, impersonal production, distribution and consumption of goods and services. This understanding is primarily based on a concern for developing and strengthening the community's wellbeing, rather than what is exchanged or the form of currency used.

negroes/lost souls act as if income, and especially spending, is a greater indicator of power than wealth. Their every economic effort is geared toward increasing their personal debt. Whether directly or not, their income and whatever little wealth they have accumulated serves to build and strengthen the businesses and personal holdings of our enemies. They even act as if others' wealth-building institutions are their own.

europeans base their whole economic order on exploitation, that is unfairly taking from the less sophisticated among their own but especially stealing the bodies, minds and resources of others. They exploit others to create whatever investments they want in their own communities. Their single-minded focus is on hoarding wealth.

Education

Afrikan nationalists know that the purpose of education is to prepare our children for survival and sovereignty. We know that there is little difference between practical and formal, specialized education in that both should work together for the purpose of securing our people's liberation. We recognize that our education never ends. It is an honorable, life-long aspiration.

negroes/lost souls think that being miseducated (learning what is useless for our liberation but praised by our enemies) and diseducated (learning to detest thinking altogether) is intelligence. They are trivia/IQ focused. At best, getting an education means passing tests, earning certificates, diplomas and other credentials so that one can get a "good job" in enemy institutions and businesses.

whites' primary purpose of schooling is to control others' access to jobs and wealth. For that reason, their educational system is designed to train others to accept, believe in and willingly contribute to their delusion of white supremacy. By design, their schooling of non-europeans condemns these victims to inferior roles (from corporate positions to prison inmates) in service to europeans.

Entertainment

Afrikan nationalists know that the western media's number one responsibility is to promote a white supremacist agenda and the european's dream of Afrikan genocide. We know that socially and economically what we get as employees in the entertainment industry is utterly insignificant in comparison to the profits europeans reap as its owners. We know that those of us who enter these arenas are either already fully compromised or are more than willing to become so in order to become a "star," to become "rich and famous." At the same time, we know that mass communication is not the european's domain only and those of us so talented have a responsibility to expend our energies edutaining our people using independent facilities, forums and voices.

negroes/lost souls see entertainment (be it sports, the stage or whatever) as an avenue to success through devoted service to those who dominate it. They are truly blind in their ambition. Their only goal is to be rich and famous, regardless of costs to their minds, bodies and souls. They are more than willing to ignore and/or dismiss any moral or ethical guidelines which would cause them to question playing roles which lower them to untold levels of self-deprecating insanity and betrayal.

europeans act as if others are here to entertain them. Accordingly, for them, all forms of entertainment are for purposes of exploiting others' talents for profit. The images they control and present in the media are designed to mold the thinking of watchers into mindless consumption. Their media is a subtle propaganda designed to make others see themselves as the inferior, impotent, ineffectual clowns europeans need them to be in order to more easily control them.

<u>Labor</u>

Afrikan nationalists work for self. We take pride in the products we create which directly contribute to our nationbuilding efforts. We work where we are needed. Regardless of talent or skill level, we apply ourselves as best we can where our nation needs us most.

negroes and lost souls are very different. Even if

they are entrepreneurs, they still work for aliens. They
live to consume the goods others manufacture and/or
market. And they do this as wastefully and conspicuously
as possible.

europeans operate on the philosophy that real work
is having others do your work for you. Laziness is a
congenital condition and high aspiration of yurugu's mind.
Their primary goal is to have others produce what they
consume for them.

Law

Afrikan nationalists focus on human rights and are fully
aware of the europeans convenient use, change and
disregard for them. We know europeans make and use
laws against us. We prioritize human (Creator given) over
civil (human given) rights. Regardless, we know that both
require enforcement, not just declarations. We understand
that yurugu's law and order is simply a means of regulating
us through a *criminal* court and prison system. We know
that justice means "just us" being locked up in today's
prisons, more accurately called the "new slave ships." We
know that the criminal justice system is criminal to the
bone. We are well aware that yurugus have broken, and
will break, every treaty and official agreement they have
made, and will make, with us without compunction and at
will.

negroes/lost souls believe that europeans believe
that their own laws are fair and justly applied to all
"citizens." They believe that europeans do not see
themselves as above the laws they create for "everyone."

These cowardly followers of criminal minds believe that justice will prevail in the west (i.e., that it is self-correcting). In order to live with themselves, the negroes/lost souls who inadvertently detect any racial bias have to delude themselves into believing that unfair laws and our greatly unequal prosecution by courts will decrease as more of us become hired as overseers in yurugu's criminal system. It is beyond them to realize that our subassimilation into this system, designed by nature to criminalize us, is a highly selective process. It only subintegrates those of us who have been dumbed down to the degree that they will be patriotic enough to believe that it can be changed while remaining the same. In other words, only those who have no desire to truly change what exists and have little to no sense of accountability to Afrikan people as a nation are invited to offices of influence.

History has clearly demonstrated that yurugus see laws as nothing more than easily changeable tools/rules for deceiving, manipulating and controlling others. They consider themselves above the law, unless it is convenient to publicly abide by them in order to gain greater domination over others later. Their laws are created based on personal and group interests, not natural or universal order.

Politics

Afrikan nationalists know that electoral politics is a joke. The vote is a ploy designed to dupe Afrikan folk into believing that they have some say in white folks' decisions. We know whose agenda rules western society, regardless of votes or figureheads. It is not within the warrior's common historical sense to believe that this is now, has ever been or will ever have the possibility of ever becoming a democracy. Instead, we understand politics as a grassroots, PanAfrikan movement, a deliberately organized social force which locally and internationally activates, concentrates and applies the collective power of our people toward visionary ends. Black nationalists define leadership based on a record of loyalty, consistency and voluntary accountability. We look more to families as leadership model, not single individuals.

In contrast to those who take history as their lesson and guide to any political order and those who created it, negroes/lost souls actually believe that this is a democracy in progress. They think that this political order is self-correcting, that the self-evident contradictions and flaws we see all around us now will somehow magically disappear sometime in the future. Moreover, they act as if they are citizens given the same rights and privileges as europeans and that western "democracy" equally serves the interests of all people under its domination. They act as if elected officials are loyal and accountable to them and strongly hold the opinion that elected officials really do serve the masses.

europeans are only interested in dominating and hoarding all resources. Politics only serves the purpose of keeping society organized so that the collection, distribution and use of resources always favors them over others. Societies they control are always politically arranged so as to manipulate others' priorities and direct their interests away from controlling their own resources in order to direct them toward meaningless, disempowered conversations and trinkets. Warriors tend to call this "politricks."

Religion

Afrikan nationalists know that religion is often a weapon used by one nation against another. We know this from our experience with christianity, islam and eastern religions. All have been used to turn our spiritual energy toward others and their gods and against us and our divinity. We also understand that organized religion is a business which reaps enormous profits from the ignorance, fear and oppression of its adherents. Warriors distinguish spirituality from religion. We recognize spirituality as our personal and national connection with the divine within us and throughout the Universe. We have a spiritual understanding of self.

negroes/lost souls actually believe that others' gods can save them. They are of the faith that europeans (and others) are the rightful intermediaries between them and divinity. And this hell they live in is made bearable, and their suffering even desirable as evidence of their undying faith, through the belief in an otherworldly paradise. The final nail in the religious coffin is their belief that, before the european's, arab's and asian's arrival, their people were without divinity.

europeans use religion as a political weapon against those they oppress and exploit. They are godless atheists at heart.

Sex

125

Afrikan nationalists know that the primary purpose of sexual intercourse is procreation. We see sex as sacred. We understand that there are clear distinctions between natural sex and the unnatural sexual behavior (misnamed sex simply because it sometimes involves sex organs) pervasive in this barbaric cave culture misnamed civilization. We know why there are boundaries separating the two. For us, sex is an expression of love between two committed, heterosexual complements.

negroes/lost souls believe that the white-sex europeans practice is the human norm. In attempting to ape this tradition, they are constantly on the hunt for anything different and unnatural to sexually enhance their spiritually deprived lives. Like their pale mentors, they look at sex as play and/or conquest. They could care less who or what is involved. In their warped desperation to be one with yurugu, they view sex with whites as the ultimate positive statement of their acceptance by them.

In the european mind, there is no separation of sex from violence. Their way of individualism and perversion require that there be no natural boundaries to "sexual" behavior. Furthermore, they see sex as a means of invading, violating and dominating others. In this bloody mind, sex is a weapon of physical and psychological control. It is a strategy of war. And, in their highly individualistic, supremacist mind, sex is only used for reproduction because of their fear of genetic annihilation.

War

Afrikan nationalists know that we are at war with a

126

determined, permanent enemy. And, because we know this, we know that forgiving and forgetting the unforgivable and unforgettable leads to even greater defeats. We know that war serves only two fundamental purposes. It is either used to subjugate/destroy others or to restore a people's freedom. We are fully aware that europeans wage war to steal others' resources and expand their empire into others' spaces. Consequently, we know that we have no choice but to accept war as the necessary avenue to the liberation of Afrikan people from foreign domination. Afrikan nationalists know that we are actually at war and that we are in this conflict for the purpose of restoring an Afrikan order.

negroes/lost souls believe that europeans wage war to spread a superior western-style democracy and to free people from tyrants and/or themselves. These blackened white patriots celebrate our participation in these wars in service to others (even against our own). They see absolutely nothing wrong with a people and their culture that violate everything. They celebrate yurugu's victories as if they are "ours" and have delusions of grandeur of becoming heroes and sheroes finally being loved by them for defending them and their corrupt, materialistic way. negroes/lost souls are more patriotic than the european to their nation and celebrate their victories even more than yurugus do.

europeans are warmongers. They proudly identify themselves as an imperialist war machine. Whether based on agriculture, manufacturing or information technology, the military-industrial complex has always been the economic, political and social foundation of their nation.

They cannot imagine life without the chaos and stress destruction brings – aggression and violence are their nature. It is one of the iceman's most prominent inheritances. War is the primary tool and excuse they use to steal others' resources.

Standing on war's frontline is the Afrikan nationalist's work. Our job is to align ourselves with our Ancestors and establish safe, secure spaces within which we can walk their path as our natural, beautiful Afrikan selves. We are here to build and defend whatever is required to help Afrikan people become sovereign.

In this effort, it is important to note that Afrikan nationalists do not engage in simple protest against oppressors, be they pickets, boycotts or any related activities. Just like simpleminded nonviolence, simple protest (a form of protest devoid of real, revolutionary action) is a problematic tactic because it is without consequence against those who work to exploit and destroy us. Simple protest is the product of weak, subintegrationist-oriented minds who believe that whites really have (or can develop) a selfless desire to solve the problems that they have intentionally created for Afrikan people.

Both simple or, rather, simpleminded protest and nonviolence are based on the belief that this viciously violent, wholly corrupted system, along with the depraved mind which created it, is reformable. They are tactics for those who do not or cannot recognize that yurugu's system is evil to its genetic core and that any adjustments or concessions it makes do not alter its predatory nature or imperialist designs.

They want reform, not revolution. And reform is

only about fighting for our subintegration into yurugu's nation without any meaningful change in its patently racist power structure. Inclusion would lessen us even more because the only possible change could be us being made more into their likeness.

This type of protest, a beggar's protest, says that you believe that what exists is basically good but that it has room for a change here and there. To complain in this way is to act with the expectation of such change, to believe you could make what is already good better. If you did not believe it could change, you would not protest it.

If you did not believe that yurugu's reality could be changed into something better, more humane, but were weak, you would ignore it. If you did not believe this, but were strong, you would leave it. But, if you did not believe this and were strong, but knew that this evil would follow you to the ends of the earth, you would destroy it.

Revolution is not reform. Afrikan nationalists do not believe this system is either correctable or good to or for anyone except members of the parasitic white nation. Therefore, we see no use for reform. Revolution is the only logical answer.

Revolution is about removing an enemy. For Afrikan warriors it is about destroying that which is evil in its entirety and replacing it with what is good and what progressively, positively works for the sanity and benefit of Black people. It is about doing whatever we need to do, mentally, physically and spiritually to bring about this complete, lasting change.

We can never forget where we are and with what we are dealing. Because we know them and know that they have no intention of ever turning control of ourselves over to us, we cannot become so blindly wishful as to think that they will allow us into their diseased fold as anything more than their mental, physical and spiritual slaves.

We would have to be even blinder to think that they would knowingly sit back while we openly organized in their midst to liberate ourselves from their domination. So it is ludicrous to think that yurugu will allow an enemy army to form in the spaces they occupy.

However, this does not mean that it cannot be done. History and ourstory repeatedly show that it can. And, each time, it was done quietly, secretly, insistently, without the oppressor's knowledge. We have done this even in the face of traitors within because the liberation of Afrikan spaces and our minds is just that important.

Afrikan nationalists who seek to build and organize in this warrior's way must overstand what they are dealing with. They must have personally grasped and sworn a blood oath of allegiance to the secrecy, diligence and persistence necessary for our eventual success. Any movement less than this is not serious.

Those who want a safe way to be revolutionary, i.e., people who, as Malcolm X said, want to claim such an honor but are "afraid to bleed," do not want revolution. Frightened impostors need to find a different, less challenging calling.

Bearing this in mind, excuses which focus our attention on our "enemy's overwhelming artillery/military superiority" have no place in a warrior's mind. A vision of sovereignty requires a total belief in its possibility. It requires an understanding of human history and the record of repeated fights against seemingly overwhelming odds that ended in victory for the underdog.

We are the underdog now. And we will not give up until we, or they, are no more. In clear sighted words, the

Last Poets reminded us of the eternal truth that it is "better to die for a noble cause than to live and die a slave." We only have two choices – either be less or become more.

Granted, being a Black nationalist can be difficult at times. Moving around and meeting hostility at virtually every turn, in almost every space, often in what seems like every face you meet, especially in those which look most like yours, can make you question the reason behind your politics and stand. It can make it seem as if there is nowhere you belong as a warrior for Afrikan people. This is the enemy's intent -- to plant doubts about success in your mind, to demoralize you, to isolate and crush you, to make it so that the battle appears lost before you even reach the frontline.

But when you are empowered in yourself, when that enemy within has been crushed, what the enemy and/or the mentacidal among us say is irrelevant relative to what you know. Rejection does no more than motivate you to even more determined action.

Clarity on these points means that we know that we cannot speak of Black nationalism outside the context of an awareness of the violation of Afrikan people. It means that we know that, first and foremost, an Afrikan nationalist is a warrior. And, without question, there is just cause for our existence.

We have risen from among a devastated people because we can no longer tolerate watching our people's pain. The insanities they act out, in conforming to their destroyer's image of them, have become too much for us to bear.

These conditions and our keen awareness of them have created us. We rise out of the ashes of destruction to destroy that destruction and secure a space for our people to rebuild our nation. We know why we're here.

Afrikan nationalists are nationbuilders. Our life's work is to establish, secure and maintain a nation. So, if you're claiming to be one, but you are not devising, building, supporting or safeguarding a program for national development, what are you surviving for? By what reason do you rationalize your existence? What gives you the right to claim a warrior's reputation or breathe a warrior's air?

The Warrior's Accountability

I align myself with the revolution, so I have to mention
That I have no time for those who seem as if they came across the word
'revolutionary' in the dictionary
And decided "oooh for the moment, this sounds like a cool thing to be"
A revolutionary state is beyond temporary
You need to wake your asses up and read our people's history
No more turning our heads from the truth so much until our necks get tired
No more sliding ass backwards down a slide into a puddle of lies into which we
must drown in
No more blissful ignorance
No more shouting for justice with just a whisper
We can no longer be a bunch of empty minds living in critical times refusing to
recognize real lies

Jasira

Order requires rules, the means to enforce them and a system of social accountability that binds members of society to each other under these rules. Rules define this order. The means of enforcement guarantees it is preserved. And a system of social accountability normalizes it.

Generally speaking, accountability is having a

personal sense of responsibility to abide by these rules and to assist in enforcing them against those members of the group who are unwilling or unable to conform to them. It is to personally feel responsible for answering to and protecting the order these rules establish.

However, for any sovereign people, accountability is much greater than just knowing a socially agreed upon set of rules and believing that all citizens should feel obligated to follow them. Having an unbreakable, unqualified loyalty to their group, and their group alone, is assumed to lie in the hearts of all group members.

Accountability, then, means to have a genuine sense of belonging to your particular group. It means that you see it as being an inseparable part of you and you as being indistinguishable from it. It requires you to believe that you have a valuable stake in the survival of your group. And it is a heartfelt duty bound by timeless, common imperatives and real (or imagined as in the case of the mentacidal) blood.

Through the eyes of nationalists, accountability requires people who sincerely feel obligated to each other for their past, present and future. They must see each other joined as one mind, body and spirit in the destiny of their lives and livelihood.

Having accountability only becomes an issue when the rewards individuals receive for being loyal originate outside their group. When they come from an external group that is oppressing and exploiting these individuals, the effects can be more than devastating.

Based on our definition of accountability and the decisive role of responsible leadership to the possibility of our people's liberation, empowerment and sovereignty, we have to conclude that the so-called leadership in the Black community lacks all sense of accountability to us. It is obvious that these "leaders" are disloyal because of their deep mentacide and the fact that their rewards and punishments originate outside the community. Sadly, for them and most lay people, there is no meaningful or permanent allegiance to The Race or each other because they have come to accept that race is irrelevant, which is nothing more than a deadly lie fostered by western, anti-Afrikan extreme individualism.

In fact, in our community, loyalty has become a liability. A self-hating allegiance to others has become so deeply ingrained in them that those of us who express any sense of racial loyalty are scoffed at as extremists and kept away from those most in need of our assistance.

We know that there are Afrikans without a sense of loyalty and obligation to us. Many who live deeply mentacidal lives in desperate search of an enemy's love demonstrate an accountability to anyone except their own. This, we know. This, we must never forget.

However, we are not mentacidal. And there is no such thing as an Afrikan nationalist without accountability, a personal obligation and duty to the people of one's nation.

Our deep sense of racial/national accountability also embraces those Ancestors who set the standard by selflessly fighting to maintain the integrity of our people. More than any other members of the Afrikan nation, we owe them. And, furthermore, because we are mentally, physically and spiritually our Ancestors, accountability is naturally built into our genes.

The word nationalist specifies nation. And a nation is a people who hold themselves accountable to each other.

Without this national sense of interpersonal responsibility we could not speak of treason. If it did not exist, any question of betrayal would automatically become, "Treason against what or whom?"

Not having concrete, indisputable physical, mental and spiritual national parameters is the single, most important factor subverting accountability among Afrikan people.   Parameters are boundaries.   These rules of contact and interaction establish unchangeable, unqualified social borders.   For good reason, they identify lines that are never to be crossed.

Parameters are the absolute borders beyond which we do not think to cross because we know they will take and keep us far outside of who we are at the core.   They mark the dividing line between those things which reflect and speak to us and those we refuse to accept as normal and natural for us simply because they are wrong.   They identify those groups of individuals who we must distance ourselves from in every way possible because they naturally corrupt the Afrikan mind, body and spirit.

Accountability requires an agreement about who we are and who or what we are not, and who we should and should not keep in our company.

Afrikan nationalists have a core set of parameters. Those which identify who we are not and what we should not do include europhilia (love of europeans), negroitis (thinking and acting as a traitor against our people) and being homosexualized (acceptance and participation in same-sex/white-sex activities).   Within a warrior's community there can be no europeans, negroes, homosexuals or promos (those who pretend not to be homosexual but defend the homosexualization of Afrikans even more fiercely than those who are openly homosexual). There is absolutely no discussion on these points for us.

Individualism, as practiced and glorified in western

society, is another major factor undermining accountability within the Black community. A single-minded focus on self makes working now for the benefit of future generations illogical. Everything is about one's immediate self for individualists. This worship of self is truly an exceedingly self-centered ideology, an interpretation of reality based on a philosophy of instant gratification. "Me-ism" rules the minds of individual Afrikans who are, for all intents and purposes, divorced from their people. Such individuals drown in their own pool of manufactured insatiable appetites, a psychological condition which could easily lead them to become traitors.

In every society, traitors are dealt with severely. For certain treasonous acts, corrections could range from ostracization to expulsion. However, the most heinous traitors receive capital punishment throughout the world. It should be no different for those who commit treason against the Afrikan nation.

However, because western society is looking for any excuse to remove us from the frontline, we have to be wise when dealing with such individuals. And we have to do this while still making an effective point to those who would follow in their treasonous footsteps.

Because the hunt is on for those of us who uncompromisingly follow the Afrikan way, we have to use common sense when correcting those who consistently and willfully betray us. It should be left up to the warrior's discretion and the opportunities available as to how to deal with a known traitor. However, it should go without saying that whatever the options or opportunities, traitors must be dealt with. No people can successfully move toward sovereignty with their traitors in tow.

All of this is to say that, whenever possible, whatever

is done must be accomplished without endangering the warrior's future contribution to our nationbuilding effort. It makes no sense for an Afrikan nationalist to remove one useless traitor only to be taken out of action, allowing many more traitors to become more effective without the nationalist's presence. We know that the european state will use these weak individuals as martyrs in its crusade for white supremacy. So, how we deal with them must be done in such a way that none of us are implicated and lost to the traitors' masters' prisons or cemeteries.

Regardless of how we deal with them, we remember these traitors for as long as they live. However, *if*, and we do mean *if*, reason is found to accept a former traitor into the Afrikan nationalist community, any repentant traitors would always be kept far away from our centers of power. They would forever be relegated to posts sitting on the periphery of nationbuilding activities. Their work must always be confined to demilitarized, non-decision-making areas.

Regardless of the seeming sincerity of their repentance, the decision to allow them to enter or return to the Afrikan nationalist fold must still be based on the severity of the treason. Only after a lifetime of extensive, dedicated, quiet nation-serving work, only after they are beyond the possibility of damaging us further, should guarded belief in their word come. During this time, they should express nothing less than an unconditionally repentant attitude, an attitude that expresses the hope that their meager contribution may somehow begin to correct for their questionable record.

Again, *if* there is good reason, they can be forgiven. However, forgetting is not an option. So, for as long as they live they should be kept from exercising any form of power or of having access to any level of information vital to national security. They have proven their disloyalty and can never, ever be trusted at the helm of any national power.

Dealing with traitors, though, is much easier than identifying them. For this reason, treason must be understood as something which happens in degrees. Anything that works against the empowerment of Afrikan people is treason to some degree or other. So, those who lie and leave the Afrikan nationalist community, as well as those who consciously work in the service of enemies to infiltrate our organizations for purposes of destroying them, can be defined as traitors. But, again, the greatest problem is in identifying who they are, hopefully before too much damage has been done.

Identification is most difficult for those intent on doing the most damage to us because they operate under a cloak of deceit. Not surprisingly, those who are the least destructive and malicious are the easiest to identify. Phonies tend to be identifiable because of laziness and the habit of repeatedly asking the same questions about things they should already understand, but rewording them in ways they hope will disguise them.

When we pay attention and listen for contradictions in their statements, we can catch the liars and gossipers because they often do not completely think about what they say before they say it and, obviously, they think they are smarter than those they lie to or they would not lie to them. Quitters, along with those whose phoniness and lies regularly catch up with them, eventually leave. This would be good if, once identified, they did not simply relocate to another nationalist community to create similar problems there.

Preventing them from constantly disrupting

valuable work could be made easier if we established a national, early warning system. All that this requires we do is select two or more very trustworthy individuals (preferably Elders) in every local nationalist community who are to be immediately notified about any individual who acts treasonously and then "disappears" with a good probability of reappearing elsewhere in conscious circles.

Regrettably, we are least able to identify the most dangerous of the treasonous because their deceit and conscious maneuverings are planned and carried out in the most underhanded of ways. They have but one intent and that is to destroy our organization and permanently remove us as a threat to their goal of white supremacy. The best defense against them is in knowing that they exist.

Even if we do not know who they are, we know that they are among us. And we should never become comfortable enough to think that they will not be around, even after we become a liberated, empowered, sovereign, feared nation, as long as there are envious, imperialistic, insecure nations like those who rule now. Enemies will always seek out the mentally and emotionally weakest among us to befriend and turn against us.

We have to be as serious about bringing new warriors in as we are in weeding out those who do not deserve our Ancestors' honor. We should only accept those with the revolutionary capacity and demonstrated interest to be Afrikan nationalists.

Though, as an army of warriors, we are correct to call these individuals civilians, they are a special breed of them. They are neither Afrikan nationalists nor negro saboteurs. However, unlike many of their chronically distracted peers, they have some idea that we are at war. Their minds will not let them forget that we have definite, relentless enemies.

It is understood, though, that Afrikan nationalists do not proselytize. All of our members should come of their own accord, from the heart. We do not corner or badger people trying to convince them they are mentacidal and convert them to our way. We are not a religion, a cult, sect or political party. We are a nation, rebuilding itself through a nationalist movement.

We "recruit" by example. We set and abide by Afrikan nationalist standards. In this way, we provide a way for aspiring warriors to be themselves. When we uncompromisingly model the warrior's standard, those who can see, who are not paralyzed by their fear of aliens and who are wise enough to move in our direction, have a beacon to approach.

We need conscious volunteers, not zombie-like, needy followers. We need individuals who can operate well within our organizations as well as lead themselves when physically isolated from other members of the nation.

We understand that there will be those in the Afrikan community who can see and those who cannot. We have no interest in wasting time and energy on those who cannot. That energy is better expended on securing and further developing what we have already established.

Therefore, our best recruitment tool is ourselves. How we carry ourselves and the strength in our belief in the possibility of a liberated, empowered, sovereign Afrikan people will attract worthy warriors. Those who come will already feel that something is horribly wrong with this reality because they sense it and see it in the eyes and deeds of our sworn enemies and the negroes and lost souls about us.

We can be content in knowing that those who come

of their own free will, who come without being talked or tricked into it, will be stronger, more focused and more determined than those who do not. And we know they have the greatest potential of all Afrikans who are not yet nationalists because being an Afrikan nationalist is the hardest of all possible choices. In this reality such a decision pits them against everything they have known to be true and takes away all sense of security in the white world.

The Warrior's Education

Revolution is War
not romance
and War is an art, not a slow dance
but a skill which requires techniques, blue prints and plans
not some bullshit debate whether I under or over stand

Wise Intelligent

Warriors are *thinking* weapons. Our minds work for us against our enemies. They use the information we supply them with to devise the best strategies and tactics to defeat and remove whatever threat crosses our paths. Because there are so many determined, evil, deceitful minds working against us, our minds have to be sharp in order to keep us alive and fully functioning as Afrikan nationalists. However, if they are not working at peak performance to build what others cannot arrest or tear down, then we will lose.

When in doubt, we have to remember that our minds are our employees. They work for us, not the other way around. In other words, your mind follows your instructions.

If you tell your mind that you are stupid, incompetent and/or unable to control your appetites, it will find a way to make these thoughts reality. It will methodically sabotage every effort you make to be more intelligent and exercise greater control over yourself. If you tell it that you are brilliant and able to do anything, then it will use everything at its disposal to make and keep you so. It will find opportunities in your every thought, word and action to guide you toward your natural genius.

So, if you are not who you need to be as the Afrikan nationalist you know you need to be, it is not your mind's fault. It is yours. Obviously, you have not adequately instructed your employee in the workings of Afrikan nationalism.

And so-called obstacles are not to blame for any failures either. As individuals of power, we cannot blame our conditions, resources, relations, past or any other convenient deterrent for what we are not doing. It is said that "Obstacles are things that you see when you take your eyes off of your goal." The greatest emphasis should be placed on "you" and "your." Only *you* can create the obstacles which block *your* mind.

There are only two choices when dealing with problems which stand in our way, whether individually or when organized with other nationalists. We can approach such circumstances or things as either lessons for self-improvement which will strengthen us as we learn and overcome them. Or, we can take the defeatist approach and see them as barriers imposed by others which are impossible to overcome and quit.

Regardless of which path we choose, the truth is that no one and nothing stands in the way of what needs to be done or you need to become, except you. Nothing stops

Afrikan nationalists but themselves.

The relevance of self-instruction to winning is found in the words of good motivational speakers. They do not tell their audience to imagine what they want to have or desire to become and, then, focus on getting it. They tell them to state what they want or want to become as if it already exists, to speak and think as if they already have it or already are it.

Using this ancient visionary, affirmative, meditative way of creative visualization, serious Afrikan nationalists would never speak of being warriors or nationbuilders as if it is something that will come to pass sometime in the future. They would never say "I will become." They speak in definite terms.

Therefore, they would say, "I *am* an Afrikan nationalist. I *am* building a sovereign ancient future. I *can never* be defeated." We speak our warriorhood into existence now, giving our minds solid, confident instructions as to the work at hand.

So, if it seems like your mind has turned on you, as if your employee is on strike or in rebellion against you, then, apparently, you have not been an effective supervisor. Apparently, you have not convinced your employee of the importance and necessity of it performing a particular task in an advantageous way. In this case, obviously, you, as the employer, have not used enough concentrated thought, creative repetition and emotional depth to impress upon your employee the need to comply with your wishes.

There is absolutely nothing, within the human possibility, that we cannot do. If there is something that is not being done it is because we do not want to do it badly enough. If we think back over our lives and that of others we know well, there has never been anything within reason that we intensely wanted which we did not receive if we worked hard enough for it.

And, there is absolutely nothing, within the human possibility, we give ourselves to do that is beyond our ability. Haven't you heard the saying that you are never given anything that you cannot handle? Spirit knows this and allocates things according to need and ability.

The only meaningful question that tends to remain unanswered until the goal is accomplished is of how long it will take. And this is mainly because we have been brought up in a reality where patience, especially with self, is not thought of as a virtue.

We have to remember, though, that most often, the length of time required for fulfillment of any passion is beyond our decision-making power. There is a simple guideline that we should keep in mind when we find ourselves concerned about how long those mental, physical, material and/or spiritual states or things we desire will take to arrive. The rule is that we receive what we are supposed to receive when we are ready to handle it correctly. Otherwise, it will be improperly handled.

Of course, if you have no desire for power, no aspiration higher than the hem of the european's skirt, then all this knowledge is meaningless. The truth is, if you are by age and race a member of the Afrikan warrior class, you are either a warrior or a pacifist. There is no safe, neutral space between the two. Since we have already discussed the warrior, we'll now turn to those who have been stripped of their warrior spirit.

Passivity, the refusal to fight even when it is called for, takes place when fear overwhelms common sense and causes us to have compassion for a relentless enemy. The frontline has not changed. The fear is just too great for the pacifist to bear. The threat and assault remain constant, except in the coward's imagination.

The lesson shown to warriors by the pacifist is that fear automatically suppresses righteous rage. And that enemies feed on our fear. It was Nana Kuntu (fka Del Jones) who reminded us that "Genocide must be fed." Afrikan nationalists can have no fear of evil, no matter how large or common it is.

Something has happened over the last half century that has weakened and even, in many ways, paralyzed the "Afrikan World Revolution." This paralysis is something we can distinctly hear in the blaring voices of those now claiming to be our scholars who, at the heart of their argument, embrace the notion that there is no "us" in Afrikan people. They would have us believe that we are more european than Afrikan, if not raceless or colorless, and that there is no permanent or significant connection between race and culture.

However, their desperate need to repeat this lie over and over again shows that they know its weakness. Most of them are not blind to their contradiction. They are quite aware of their privileged role as the intellectual pastors of a community of sheep. They know they shepherd a paranoid flock whose lives center around their fears of attracting the wrong attention from a pack of insatiable, pale wolves. Their security and privilege come from reassuring a flock whose greatest desire is simply to graze on the toxic grass of passive inferiority in peace.

Because this is a white reality, in the official academic sectors of the Afrikan community these compromised voices carry the greatest weight. Unknown before, they have risen to fill the vacuum left as our master teachers transitioned -- Clarke, Wilsons, Jehewty (Carruther), Kuntu

(Jones) and others who lived and died for their people. Like the weak kings of Kemet issued in its decline from global grace and power, today's subservient mouthpieces intentionally misrepresent our traditions, beliefs, way and vision so that they will mirror those of the europeans. They have put all their energies into distorting and falsifying what it means to be Afrikan, so much so that it appears european.

These are not the educators of Afrikan nationalists. Our educators are Afrikan nationalists themselves. They know who we are and what we need to know and do to create a sovereign nation. They have dedicated their lives to the upliftment and empowerment of Afrikan people. Arming the vanguard of warriors who do this work with the best artillery they can muster out of the barrel of their pens is their calling.

We call these seasoned frontline thinkers Jegna, an Ethiopian (Amharic) concept Wade W. Nobles defined so well for us. They

...are those special people who have (1) been tested in struggle or battle, (2) demonstrated extraordinary and unusual fearlessness, (3) shown determination and courage in protecting her/his people, land and culture, (4) shown diligence and dedication to our people, (5) produced an exceptionally high quality of work, and (6) dedicated themselves to the protection, defense, nurturance and development of our young by advancing our people, place and culture.

We do not call them mentor because that is a lesser, homosexual concept.

Because these masters are human, though, they have made and will make mistakes. But, in the scheme of things, those errors in judgment do not make a contradiction of them. These errors are small. Moreover, their personal lives do not make a lie of their professional/public statements.

A Jegna is unlike any of those loud individuals who have somehow managed to become elevated in our eyes because they speak so dramatically and authoritatively about warriorhood, but who live pacified, dysfunctional lives. What Afrikans of this caliber say and think is who they actually are. Our master warriors are not fictions of Afrikan man- or womanhood, images which ultimately serve our enemy's way of thinking. In thought, word and deed, they are the epitome of Afrikan warriorhood.

How do evolving Afrikan nationalists learn what they need to know to become master warriors? We read, study and think politically. We learn what we need to know from (1) the formal instruction of those ahead of us (being in their presence and deeply considering what they have to offer us); (2) reading/studying the materials we discover or have been led to along our way (self-instruction); (3) meditation (taking the time to be still and listening to what comes from inside the Universe) and (4) experience (life in general and through applied work).

Regardless of which form or forms our education comes in, we are thinking weapons because we study only that which is relevant to the work we are here to do. Chancellor Williams told us that we cannot afford to read and interpret just to be reading and interpreting. He warned us about intellectualizing while under assault.

What we study of the past must show us where we must go and what we must change to get there. As John Henrik Clarke schooled us, ourstory (and others' history relative to it) is our clock and compass, telling us what time it is and the direction we must take to return to greatness.

He also told us that if anything we have does not

serve a revolutionary purpose we must cast it aside. Everything that we mentally digest must be turned into the type of artillery that can more decisively revolutionize our minds into greater weapons against our enemies.

Again, warriors are *thinking* weapons. Therefore, what we read must be studied specifically for its usefulness on the frontline. If it does not contribute to our understanding of what it means to be an Afrikan warrior actively engaged in the nationbuilding process, it should be "discarded."

Every statement we read and hear is political. It reflects a particular worldview. And every worldview reflects a given people's interests and interpretation of reality. When this is clearly understood, Afrikan nationalists make the time to define or redefine every word they speak in Afrikan centered, nationbuilding terms. Otherwise, we are contradicting ourselves because we cannot use our enemies' definitions to properly explain ourselves or clearly identify them.

The following reading list is a sampling of those critical books Afrikan nationalists need to read and study in order to find their way through the political minefields of western literature.

Balogun O. Abeegunde, *Afrikan Martial Arts: Discovering the Warrior Within*
Kwame Agyei Akoto, *Nationbuilding*
The American Directory of Certified Uncle Toms
Fundi Sanyika Anwisye, *The African Personality: Lubrication for Liberation*
Ayi Kwei Armah, *Two Thousand Seasons*
N. Xavier Arnold, *The Genocide Files*
Mwalimu K. Bomani Baruti, *Kebuka!: Remembering the*

Middle Passage Through the Eyes of Our Ancestors and *IWA: A Warrior's Character*
Jacob H. Carruther, *The Irritated Genie*
John Henrik Clarke, *Who Betrayed the African World Revolution*
Marcus Garvey, *Message to the People: The Course of African Philosophy*
Irritated Genie, *War on the Horizon*
Sam Greenlee's *The Spook Who Sat by the Door*
Hubert Henry Harrison, *When Africa Awakes*
Asa G. Hilliard, *The Maroon Within Us*
Del Jones, *The Afrikan Holocaust* and *Afrikan Holocaust 2000*
Kamau R. Kambon, *Afrikan Guerrilla Warfare In amerika*
Shawna Maglangbayan, *Garvey, Lumumba and Malcolm: Afrikan National-Separatists*
Tony Martin, *Race First*
Clarence J. Munford, *Race and Reparations*
The Nation of Islam, *The Secret Relationship Between Afrikans and Jews*
Alphonso Pinkney, *Red, Black and Green: Black nationalism in the United States*
George S. Schuyler's *Afrikan Empire*
Esmeralda Simmons, "Parable of the Africans and the Foreign Oasis" (in Mwalimu K. Bomani Baruti, *Notes Toward Higher Ideals in Afrikan Intellectual Liberation*)
Elleni Tedla, *Sankofa: African Thought & Education*
Harriet A. Washington, *Medical Apartheid*
Frances Cress Welsing, *The Isis Papers*
Chancellor Williams, *The Destruction of Afrikan Civilization: Great Issues of a Race from 4500 B.C. to 2000 A.D.*
Robert F. Williams, *Negroes with Guns*
Amos N. Wilson, *Afrikan-Centered Consciousness versus The*

151

New World Order and *Blueprint for Afrikan Power*
Carter G. Woodson, *The Miseducation of the Negro*
Bobby E. Wright, *The Psychopathic Racial Personality and other essays*

Again, recognize that these are only a few of the books that we need to study if we are to reach our full conscious potential on the frontline.

Work is critical. But study gives work intelligent, knowledgeable direction.

The Warrior's Religion

In fear of being Afrikan and standing for our people
We run and seek shelter under church corner steeples....
If in fear of the devil you ran toward religion
Fear should not have been the basis for your decision

Precise Science

Whether we call our beliefs about The Creator and divinity religion or spirituality, it is supposed to define the way we *live*, inside and out. Our interpretation of a higher power or mind within us and throughout the Universe is supposed to be reflected, without contradiction, in how we think and speak and act toward ourselves, each other, other humans, animals, Earth and the Universe itself. These beliefs should be clearly evident in our approach to things and resources. And they should manifest themselves in the technology we choose, use and advance in the interests of our people, as well as that which we may reluctantly develop but necessarily use against those who would destroy us.

What we believe is the reason for being and how that belief is reflected in our daily lives is our religion/spirituality. It is what we would call our belief system. And, whether we are aware that we have a belief system or not, it is present in our every thought, word and deed.

However, the contradictory or evil nature of so many people around us may cause us to doubt this. But, we have to remember where we are. This is a spirit deprived, willfully deceitful reality.

We also have to remember that no one said that a religious/spiritual system has to see reality in good or humane terms. There is no rule that says that a belief system has to hold human life higher than material possessions. That is usually the thinking of naive idealists who believe in the humanity of every person or people and conveniently forget the kind of people who now dominate this world.

Many become confused on this point because of the fictional respect for humanity found in the laws, writings and heroes of the national religions of europeans, arabs and asians. But, as with any modern assessment of a people, we have to look at what has occurred since their beginning to get a real understanding of their true nature and intent.

History is the key. History reveals contradiction or denies it, for, regardless of what a people may now say about who or what they are, history allows us to see what or who they have always been.

Before anything else, we have to understand that religion is a political weapon. When we study "world" religions, we can easily see that others' religions and our spirituality have been aggressively and violently used against us for thousands of years in an attempt to steal everything we have and are.

An extremely important point here is that we cannot allow ourselves to get caught up in debates about religious origins. In the final analysis, it makes no difference whether all the world's religions originated in Afrikan or not. Origin is an irrelevant piece of the nationalist's knowledge when our focus is correctly directed toward their systematic (intentional and continuous) use by our enemies against us.

Therefore, the most important question for Afrikan nationalists is not the origins of religions but how have these institutions have been practiced against Afrikan people. Nothing else about them is relevant until that influence is understood, checked and removed.

Of course, as difficult as it can make our lives, we must remain aware that many of those who look like us who practice these religions are necessarily disloyal to the PanAfrikan nation because this is what these religions demand. And, for this reason, their religious affiliations remain a serious concern for us.

Simply put, any religion which is controlled by our enemies, and practiced by those who look like us who believe in white or off-white gods, has no place in any Afrikan nationalist's spiritual space. Like alien, anti-Afrikan political, economic, educational, familial and military systems, they are the political tools of their masters. They have been formed or retooled to fit their agenda, and their agenda alone. And, since their masters see us as an enemy who must be destroyed, these tools have been used against us accordingly.

Again, even if their rules and structure at first came from Afrika, exported religions have been severely modified to fit another people's mind and personality. They are no longer Afrikan.

It is a social fact that a people and their culture mold their religious, political, economic, familial and other institutional forms to fit their personality and interests, not the other way around.

As George G.M. James pointed out in *Stolen Legacy*, this is why Socrates had to be killed. He tried to bring the Afrikan way of thinking into european society, but they wanted the intellectual technology, not the spirit that accompanied it.

In the end, there is no reason to ignore the fact that to know things in their purest form we always need to go back as far as is humanly possible into their origins. Acknowledging this, if we are to be our spiritual selves, we have to study and practice that which originated among Black people in traditional and classical Afrikan societies. We need to study and practice the spiritual systems of our people, among ourselves only, in the way that our ancient Ancestors did. What reason, outside of fear and ignorance, would make us settle for some mutated version of Afrikan spirituality?

In short, we should again note that the vast majority of Afrikan folk practicing european, arab and asian style religions have no loyalty whatsoever to us. Their allegiances lie in the Vatican, Jerusalem, Mecca or asian holy places, anywhere but the Afrikan continent. There is nothing holy about any place in Afrika to them, unless it is first approved by their enemies.

However, if there are Afrikans who are personally practicing an alien or alienated religious system in order to better discipline their spirits in service to Afrikan people, Afrikans who are Afrikan nationalist in thought, word and deed, they should not be penalized for doing so. However, if they say they are Afrikan, then the contradiction of claiming (even if in name only) the religion of enemies in the presence of a purer ancestral form, should be brought to their attention.

There is no room for christianity, islam, buddhism,

hinduism or whatever in the Afrikan nationalist movement unless those religions are specifically used to serve the revolutionary interests of Afrikan people and assist us in arresting and destroying our enemies.

To save confusion, this also applies to Afrikan spiritual systems practiced by mentacidal, eurocentric Afrikans. In this case, in fact, many of these individuals are even worse enemies to us because they know exactly what they are doing, however they choose to rationalize it. They are intentionally using what is ours to aid others against us.

The Warrior's Rules

something inside of me guiding me
keeps reminding me -- to rewind and see
no following blindly/the worst is behind me
every cell of my being/responding to freedom

staHHr

The following summary statements describe the imperatives and character of Afrikan nationalists. They are written as and should be read as affirmations of who we are and what we are not.

- *I have an unqualified love and respect for my/our children, complement, fellow warriors and Elders.*
- *I believe in our "Race First."*
- *I do not sleep with my enemies. I have no white (or other nonAfrikan) bed partners and do not procreate with them.*
- *I am strictly heterosexual. I neither condone, support nor promote sexual insanity.*
- *I am not an interracialist. I do not have "white friends."*
- *I do not associate with enemies unless my survival depends on it.*
- *I look to the wisdom of my Ancestors and Elders for direction.*

- I am prepared for any exigency.

- I dress for war not display. A traditional sense of decency always guides my appearance.

- I daily listen to consciousness raising, revolutionary music.

- I am a thinker, not an intellectual. I apply what I know.

- I am deeply spiritual (not religious).

- I do not align myself with enemy based (communist/socialist/internationalist) organizations.

- I am not and do not associate with feminists.

- I uncompromisingly work toward the complete and total liberation, empowerment and sovereignty of Afrikan people.

- I am not contradictory in what I think, say and do.

- I am resilient. I never give up.

Final Thoughts

It is a myth that we share this planet. Sharing requires some degree of equality. Sharing is a mutual action between two or more individuals, groups or nations who respect each other. We do not share this planet. europeans dominate it and us. They share nothing of worth.

No matter how painful or angering this truth may feel to warriors, we have to spiritually comprehend this glaring fact if we are ever going to build anything of substance again. As we face a knowledgeable, determined, aggressive, hateful opposition, building requires knowing who and what they are so that effective measures can be taken to prevent them from hindering our construction. This we must grasp and accept if we are to build for eternity.

While there are people who are holding their own

against the european, we are not among them. And we are not concerned with them, if for no other reason than being concerned with them drains our energy into their cause, leaving us more open to their exploitation of us. We live in our own special hell, in spaces and a reality ruled by the iron fist of a selfish, intolerant, hateful, greedy, predatory people. Our role and situation here is unique and without rival.

Yurugu, the beings ("people" being an identity they have never deserved) who are our primary focus, are really quite easy to understand. Three interrelated factors reveal all a warrior needs to begin grasping a necessary solution to our problem.

First, even a limited historical observation tells us that *they cannot allow any of the people they have conquered and destroyed, or are otherwise being destroyed through subassimilation into their societies, to be themselves.* These insecure beings cannot permit this even in others' own spaces because of their psychopathic fear of others waking up to what has been done, and is being done to them, and the power that they have been forced to hide from themselves. Yurugu knows that their victims' awakening will surely cause them to lose their ill-gotten, undeserved privilege in this world. Add to this fact that they consider *all* spaces theirs, and we can more fully understand this mentality.

The second factor is that *they cannot allow any people to operate independent of them.* Their supremacist-imperialist desire and racist arrogance cannot allow them to conceive of a world where other people exist in sovereignty beyond their control or manipulation. The insatiable greed and incessantly nagging insecurities, born in the caves in which they discovered themselves, make the idea of anyone living on the planet outside of their authority and validation unthinkable. In their warped, childish imaginations, no

162

reality that they exist in can operate efficiently without them being in the position of absolute and total domination over everyone else.

The third factor is that *we cannot be our Afrikan selves within european culture and society.* To be Afrikan requires us to be everything that their world cannot allow because it is violently anti-Afrikan to its core. And it is not possible to change it into something more receptive to differences in worldview and interpretation of reality. It is incapable of tolerating difference.

In these three facts lie the warrior's only reasonable line of thinking and choice. For, (1) if europeans cannot allow anyone to be themselves in their space, (2) if they cannot allow anyone to exist outside their sphere of power and (3) if we cannot be who we naturally are within their space, then we really do not have any choices if we are to be free. If we are to be Afrikan in the world as it is (an impossibility for us in european space, and europeans consider all spaces theirs), if we are to be our natural selves, if we are to become a liberated, empowered, sovereign people, we only have the choices of removing them (permanently or through secured isolation) or removing ourselves (permanently or through secured isolation). Nothing less will permit us to be Afrikan.

Yurugu's haunting memories and justified fears have caused our righteous rage to awaken and rise. Without our historical, inhuman violation by them, there would be no need for Afrikan nationalists. Oppression brings forth revolutionaries.

We are the defenders of a people turned into this world's scavengers – beggars for power, a home, an identity but who voluntarily wallow in their own and others' waste.

All of these, our power, our home, our identity, have always been where they are now, within. We have just allowed others to turn our eyes away from us.

Doing this work is extremely difficult and, at this time, mostly unrewarded. It requires a special kind of warrior, a special kind of Afrikan man and a special kind of Afrikan woman, to hold this vision and fulfill this mission. It requires a disciplined, focused, righteous character. And it is work that cannot be successfully completed without minds knowledgeable of our ancestral direction.

There can be no individualized egos here. Vanity and pride have no place. We are not trying to become celebrated sheroes or heroes. We are not looking for false pedestals on which to elevate ourselves above the masses. There is only purpose, a higher calling grounded in the vision of building the Afrikan nation into a fully liberated, empowered, sovereign nation again, one final time, forever.

We are here to remove our people from this madness or, rather, offer them the real opportunity to remove this madness from themselves. We are here to provide them with ample space and freedom to realize themselves. We are here to guarantee them the chance to be our Ancestors in all their essence and creative genius. We are not the lords of our people. We are their servants.

This is an enormous responsibility. And keeping this vision in sight, as well as the insecurities of those we recognize as aliens in mind, we have been left with but one solution – revolutionary independent, Afrikan centered nationbuilding.

We have tried everything else, peace, love, prayer, sacrifice, silence, subintegration, subassimilation, subamalgamation, suicide and been left wanting. As generally applied in our efforts to regain our human dignity,

164

these are no longer strategically intelligent options for warriors on the frontlines.

Of course, the problem is in what we, as a people, want. And far too many of us want nothing more than to be accepted and loved by a determined enemy because we feel they are superior and that we cannot visualize or build anything without them.

This nightmare of submissive invisibility in hell is definitely not the Afrikan nationalist's dream. As we have stated many times already, the Black nationalist wants nothing less than the complete and final liberation, empowerment and sovereignty of Black people.

So, again, given the power, determination and success of our opposition, regaining our sanity and rightful place in this world as a nation of people can only be accomplished through the concerted efforts of our Afrikan nationalists. In this nationbuilding solution there are four primary, interconnected aspects:

(1) character transformation of warriors and, then, through example and guidance, the masses;

(2) removal of europeans and any others who threaten our existence – the only two real options for this "removal," have been indicated above;

(3) systematic (political/formal) organization building within a nexus of international centers; and

(4) reclaiming/regaining absolute control over the properties of our physical, intellectual and spiritual selves:
a) intellectual properties include our interpretation of science and reality, ourstorical analysis

165

and conclusions about the past and present with an eye on a dynamic, progressive Afrikan future,

b) physical properties include resource (which include people) and spatial (land, infrastructure, facilities/building) properties, and

- and spiritual properties include peace within and between us, a definition of the Creator in our image and connection with creative force within, the entirety of Afrika as our holy land, the formal establishment of people's shrines, such as the Kemetic (misnamed Atlantic) Ocean, and national reverence for our warrior Ancestors.

Accomplishing one of these without the others will not work. All are required to establish and maintain nationhood. And no one is better qualified to take on this phenomenal PanAfrikan nationbuilding project than the Afrikan nationalist.

Akoben House Order Form

Please send:

_____ copies of *Message To The Warriors* ($19.95 each) $ _____

_____ copies of *IWA* ($24.95 each) $ _____

_____ copies of *Centered* ($16.95 each) $ _____

_____ copies of *Yurugu's Eunuchs* ($16.95 each) $ _____

_____ copies of *Revolutionary Daily Thoughts* ($19.95 each) $ _____

_____ copies of *Sesh* ($16.95 each) $ _____

_____ copies of *Eureason* ($19.95 each) $ _____

_____ copies of *Higher Ideals* ($16.95 each) $ _____

_____ copies of *Battle Plan* ($12.95 each) $ _____

_____ copies of *Kebuka!* ($15.95 each) $ _____

_____ copies of *Mentacide and other essays* ($16.95each) $ _____

_____ copies of *Asafo* ($19.95 each) $ _____

_____ copies of *Complementarity* ($14.95 each) $ _____

_____ copies of *Homosexuality and the Effeminization of Afrikan Males* ($24.95 each) $ _____

_____ copies of *The Sex Imperative* ($16.00 each) $ _____

_____ copies of *Excuses, Excuses* ($13.00 each) $ _____

_____ copies of *negroes and other essays* ($13.00 each) $ _____

_____ copies of *Chess Primer* ($12.95 each) $ _____

Shipping & Handling: $ _____
($6 for 1 book and $4 for each additional book.)

TOTAL ENCLOSED: $ _____

NAME: _____

ADDRESS: _____

E-mail (Optional): _____

Send this order form, along with your check or money order
(made payable to AKOBEN), to:

Akoben House, P.O. Box 10786, Atlanta, GA 30310
or order by credit card at
www.AkobenHouse.com

Made in the USA
Columbia, SC
29 July 2020

14845223R10098